W9-AVR-972

OPPOSING
VIEWPOINTS®
SERIES

Free Trade

Other Books of Related Interest:

At Issue Series

Do Schools Prepare Students for a Global Economy?

Does the World Hate the United States?

Current Controversies Series

Developing Nations

Importing from China

Global Viewpoints Series

Capitalism

Workers' Rights

Introducing Issues with Opposing Viewpoints Series

Labor Unions

"Congress shall make no law . . . abridging the freedom of speech, or of the press."

First Amendment to the US Constitution

The basic foundation of our democracy is the First Amendment guarantee of freedom of expression. The Opposing Viewpoints series is dedicated to the concept of this basic freedom and the idea that it is more important to practice it than to enshrine it.

Free Trade

Ann Aubrey Hanson and Lynn M. Zott, Book Editors

GREENHAVEN PRESS
A part of Gale, Cengage Learning

Detroit • New York • San Francisco • New Haven, Conn • Waterville, Maine • London

Elizabeth Des Chenes, *Director, Publishing Solutions*

For more information, contact:
Greenhaven Press
27500 Drake Rd.
Farmington Hills, MI 48331-3535
Or you can visit our Internet site at gale.cengage.com

Articles in Greenhaven Press anthologies are often edited for length to meet page requirements. In addition, original titles of these works are changed to clearly present the main thesis and to explicitly indicate the author's opinion. Every effort is made to ensure that Greenhaven Press accurately reflects the original intent of the authors. Every effort has been made to trace the owners of copyrighted material.

Cover image copyright © Ian McKinnell/Photographer's Choice/Getty Images.

LIBRARY OF CONGRESS CATALOGING-IN-PUBLICATION DATA

Free trade / Ann Aubrey Hanson and Lynn M. Zott, book editors.
    p. cm. -- (Opposing viewpoints)
    Includes bibliographical references and index.
    ISBN 978-0-7377-6054-5 (hbk.) -- ISBN 978-0-7377-6055-2 (pbk.)
    1. Free trade. I. Hanson, Ann Aubrey. II. Zott, Lynn M. (Lynn Marie), 1969-
    HF1713.F73534 2013
    382'.71--dc23

                                      2012035629

Printed in the United States of America
1 2 3 4 5   17 16 15 14 13

Contents

Chapter 3: What Is the Effect of Free Trade on Human Rights and Labor Regulations?

Chapter 4: What Are Some Issues Surrounding Free Trade and the Global Marketplace?

Why Consider Opposing Viewpoints?

> *"The only way in which a human being can make some approach to knowing the whole of a subject is by hearing what can be said about it by persons of every variety of opinion and studying all modes in which it can be looked at by every character of mind. No wise man ever acquired his wisdom in any mode but this."*
>
> John Stuart Mill

In our media-intensive culture it is not difficult to find differing opinions. Thousands of newspapers and magazines and dozens of radio and television talk shows resound with differing points of view. The difficulty lies in deciding which opinion to agree with and which "experts" seem the most credible. The more inundated we become with differing opinions and claims, the more essential it is to hone critical reading and thinking skills to evaluate these ideas. Opposing Viewpoints books address this problem directly by presenting stimulating debates that can be used to enhance and teach these skills. The varied opinions contained in each book examine many different aspects of a single issue. While examining these conveniently edited opposing views, readers can develop critical thinking skills such as the ability to compare and contrast authors' credibility, facts, argumentation styles, use of persuasive techniques, and other stylistic tools. In short, the Opposing Viewpoints Series is an ideal way to attain the higher-level thinking and reading skills so essential in a culture of diverse and contradictory opinions.

In addition to providing a tool for critical thinking, Opposing Viewpoints books challenge readers to question their own strongly held opinions and assumptions. Most people form their opinions on the basis of upbringing, peer pressure, and personal, cultural, or professional bias. By reading carefully balanced opposing views, readers must directly confront new ideas as well as the opinions of those with whom they disagree. This is not to argue simplistically that everyone who reads opposing views will—or should—change his or her opinion. Instead, the series enhances readers' understanding of their own views by encouraging confrontation with opposing ideas. Careful examination of others' views can lead to the readers' understanding of the logical inconsistencies in their own opinions, perspective on why they hold an opinion, and the consideration of the possibility that their opinion requires further evaluation.

Evaluating Other Opinions

To ensure that this type of examination occurs, Opposing Viewpoints books present all types of opinions. Prominent spokespeople on different sides of each issue as well as well-known professionals from many disciplines challenge the reader. An additional goal of the series is to provide a forum for other, less known, or even unpopular viewpoints. The opinion of an ordinary person who has had to make the decision to cut off life support from a terminally ill relative, for example, may be just as valuable and provide just as much insight as a medical ethicist's professional opinion. The editors have two additional purposes in including these less known views. One, the editors encourage readers to respect others' opinions—even when not enhanced by professional credibility. It is only by reading or listening to and objectively evaluating others' ideas that one can determine whether they are worthy of consideration. Two, the inclusion of such viewpoints encourages the important critical thinking skill of objectively evaluating an author's credentials and bias. This evaluation will illuminate an author's reasons for taking a particular stance on an issue and will aid in readers' evaluation of the author's ideas.

It is our hope that these books will give readers a deeper understanding of the issues debated and an appreciation of the complexity of even seemingly simple issues when good and honest people disagree. This awareness is particularly important in a democratic society such as ours in which people enter into public debate to determine the common good. Those with whom one disagrees should not be regarded as enemies but rather as people whose views deserve careful examination and may shed light on one's own.

Thomas Jefferson once said that "difference of opinion leads to inquiry, and inquiry to truth." Jefferson, a broadly educated man, argued that "if a nation expects to be ignorant and free . . . it expects what never was and never will be." As individuals and as a nation, it is imperative that we consider the opinions of others and examine them with skill and discernment. The Opposing Viewpoints series is intended to help readers achieve this goal.

David L. Bender and Bruno Leone,
Founders

Introduction

"The freedom to trade is a necessary adjunct to private property rights. A secure right to property means little if people are not permitted to exchange their property for other property they desire more. This is the essence of trade. International trade organizations, protracted debates about globalization, and convoluted trade agreements have turned the field of international trade into a complex matter, but trade is, at its root, simply an exchange between two parties who both stand to benefit."

—Robert A. Sirico,
Defending the Free Market:
The Moral Case for a Free Economy

Under strict free trade practices, prices of goods and services are dictated by supply and demand rather than by government price setting or allocation. Free trade implies the trading of goods or services without taxes or other trade barriers; the absence of "trade-distorting" policies such as taxes, subsidies, regulations, or laws that give one group an advantage over another in the market; free access to markets and market information; and freedom from government-imposed monopolies.

Those who support free trade believe that suppliers should be allowed to create and develop their own markets without government interference. Those who oppose free trade believe that governments should enact restrictions and guidelines in the market—to protect vulnerable industries or to "level the playing field" by enabling smaller companies to be competitive with larger companies. These are not new arguments; they have likely been around for as long as trade has existed.

Trade records exist from as early as the nineteenth century BCE, documenting the existence of an Assyrian merchant colony in Cappadocia, which is in present-day Turkey. Later records illustrate trade in the Far East, Arabia, India, Africa, the Middle East, and eventually—due to the expansion of the Roman Empire—across what is present-day Europe. As Europeans set sail across the globe, new trade routes were established and trade became worldwide. Trade at this point was expansive and unrestricted by governments.

In 1799 the Dutch East India Company, formerly the world's largest company, went bankrupt, partly due to the rise of competitive free trade. Now there were many companies trading in the global marketplace, and competition was fierce. Governments began to make restrictions and regulations on trade in an attempt to give an advantage to their specific nations, protect their nations from what they perceived as unfair competition, and establish favorable trade for themselves. In 1840 Britain invaded China to overturn the Chinese ban on opium imports. Governments turned to war in an effort to secure products in lieu of trade agreements.

Many early economists, such as Adam Smith and David Ricardo, believed that free trade was the reason why certain civilizations prospered economically. But there were others who opposed free trade and pushed for government control of trade; this was known as mercantilism. This argument continues to this day, as free trade proponents have battled with mercantilists, protectionists, isolationists, communists, populists, and other believers in regulation.

In the early half of the nineteenth century, the United States, a newcomer to global trade, signed an agreement with Siam—the Treaty of Amity and Commerce Between Siam and the United States—calling for free trade, except for export of rice and import of armaments. A free trade agreement was finalized in 1860 between Britain and France that initiated similar agreements between other countries in Europe. In 1868 Japan opened its borders for free trade, and bilateral treaties forbade restraint of trade imports to Japan.

However, as the US economy and other world economies staggered—during the Long Depression in Europe that started at the end of the 1800s and through the Great Depression in the United States that began in 1929—the call grew stronger for protectionism as worried citizens clamored for economic regulations to strengthen their own domestic industries against lower prices abroad.

In 1944 and 1947, respectively, the Bretton Woods system and the General Agreement on Tariffs and Trade were enacted to prevent further depressions and to rationalize trade among nations. Even then, institutions and rules to prevent trade barriers were included in the agreements as most economists argued that the lack of free trade had proven to be a principal cause of war. In the decades that followed, nations banded together—for example, in the European Economic Community in 1958 and the European Free Trade Association in 1960—to create level playing fields for trade and global commerce.

Throughout the history of trade, many nations—some of them vocal proponents of free trade today—had significant barriers to trade throughout their history. Some degree of protectionism is the norm throughout the world, but as the global marketplace changes with the advent of communication and travel, the economic playing field is also changing. Every nation is carefully considering the pros and cons of free trade and protectionism to decide how best to succeed in the twenty-first century.

Many facets of the controversy surrounding free trade are examined in *Opposing Viewpoints: Free Trade*, in chapters titled How Does Free Trade Affect the US Economy?, How Does Free Trade Impact Developing Countries?, What Is the Effect of Free Trade on Human Rights and Labor Regulations?, and What Are Some Issues Surrounding Free Trade and the Global Marketplace? With expanding ease of communication and transportation between nations, these issues will continue to be of great importance in the coming decades.

CHAPTER 1

How Does Free Trade Affect the US Economy?

Chapter Preface

The United States is engaged in a global economy, and commerce does not stop at the nation's borders. Engaging in the world market means engaging in trade with other nations, and how the United States engages in trade with these economies determines the economic strength and viability of America. Weak or bad trade policies can harm the economic health of the United States, whereas strong and clear-sighted economic trade policies can protect and improve the US economy.

One crucial question is how do free trade and protectionism affect the value of the US dollar, and by extension the purchasing power of the average American?

In the past three decades, the US dollar—the benchmark for world currency—has been on a seesaw, declining in value during one decade and gaining value during another. In the decade of the 2010s, the dollar is weak. This weakened dollar is a detriment to US consumers and US companies that import products from other countries, since a weak dollar can buy less. When the dollar is weak, US citizens have less buying power and must pay more for the items they purchase. A weak dollar typically means that Americans spend less, and the economy suffers as the nation waits out the dollar-value decline. On the other hand, a weakening US dollar benefits other players in the world marketplace. The weak dollar encourages foreign manufacturers to establish factories in the United States, bringing with these factories jobs and other economic benefits. It also encourages foreign buyers to purchase US goods at "lower" prices in their currency. So, while Americans tend to buy fewer American and import products when the dollar is weak, foreign consumers buy more US products. This sets up a trade imbalance. Trade imbalances are not necessarily bad, but too large an imbalance is unsustainable, and in the long run, the US economy will suffer.

There is a delicate balance of dollar valuation that must be achieved to protect the US consumer and producer while opening doors to global trading markets. In September 1985, the US dollar was so strong compared to other world currencies that on September 22, "government officials from five nations, the United States, France, the United Kingdom, West Germany and Japan, met in the Plaza Hotel in New York City to sign a definitive agreement to work toward US dollar devaluation," according to Jeffrey Snider on the website RealClearMarkets. In the ensuing two years, central banks used $10 billion to force the dollar's value lower, primarily targeting the intervention on Japan, where the yen was weak. The German mark was also a minor target.

The devaluation was so successful that it led to another historic accord in February 1987, signed at the Louvre in Paris, France, aimed at undoing some of the excess of the Plaza Accord. "It was feared that if the dollar continued to fall much further, it would trigger a rise in US interest rates, derailing the economic expansion that was, at that point, becoming more uneven than the first stages of the recovery from the 1982–83 recession. Other members of the G6 [an unofficial group of the interior ministers of six European Union member states with the largest populations] were also wary of the trade implications of an overly weak dollar," explained Snider.

Free trade should lead to bilateral trade mechanisms that create real productivity for both parties. But some commentators point out that trade as it has developed especially in the past three decades is unilateral, whereby marginal trade is returned in the form of some financial instrument rather than a reciprocal good. As Snider explains, "In our current set of arrangements, we see unilateral arrangement after unilateral arrangement . . . there is true wealth creation only on one side of the trade. In reality, foreign counterparties saw growing true, productive wealth while the US has seen growing financial 'wealth.' The US has piled up trillions in paper while trade partners pile up productive capacity." He continues, "Free trade throughout the 1990s and 2000s was the embodiment of the proverbial free lunch. Except there is no free lunch, not even when you control the printing press and the keys to unfettered fractional credit production. For all that has happened since 1985, and all that was intended to happen, imported goods rule the marginal economy to a degree never imagined back then, no matter where the dollar has traded during the interim. While large businesses have changed their tune about the devalued dollar, the public on both sides have little to show for it."

The value of the US dollar is one aspect of free trade that affects the US economy. The authors of the viewpoints in the following chapter of *Opposing Viewpoints: Free Trade* also focus on the impact of free trade on the American job market; whether free trade is the best course of action to spur US economic recovery; how free trade influences the US position in the global marketplace; and whether trade protections should be in place to support US manufacturing.

> *"Free trade agreements . . . are urgently needed. Despite a popular view that open trade kills American jobs, the particulars of these agreements show their benefits."*

Free Trade Boosts US Exports and Creates American Jobs

Bill Reinsch

Bill Reinsch is president of the National Foreign Trade Council and serves as a member of the US-China Economic and Security Review Commission. In the following viewpoint, Reinsch explains the benefits to the US economy of the signing of three free trade agreements with Colombia, Panama, and South Korea, respectively. He asserts that such trade agreements will help the US economy by increasing exports and creating and supporting tens of thousands of jobs. Reinsch contends that Congress has made the mistake in the past of allowing public opinion against free trade to guide its policy decisions rather than basing policies on sound economic facts. Having learned from unjust trade agreements that hurt the US economic sector in the past, Congress has, Reinsch maintains, ensured that these new agreements contain provisions that allow the parties to combat unfair practices.

As you read, consider the following questions:

1. By how many billions of dollars is the Colombia free trade agreement expected to help the US economy grow, according to the viewpoint?

2. The extension of what waterway, according to Reinsch, is expected to help boost US sales, exports, and employment opportunities for American workers?

3. What does Reinsch say is the reason for the public's skepticism regarding these three FTAs?

Finally, after more than four years of debate and acrimony, Congress is expected to pass the free trade agreements the United States negotiated with Colombia, Panama, and South Korea. All three will go a long way in helping to give a much-needed boost to the economy by increasing US exports and supporting and creating tens of thousands of American jobs.

For those of us who speak for hundreds of US companies with thousands of workers and worldwide operations, these free trade agreements (or FTAs) are urgently needed. Despite a popular view that open trade kills American jobs, the particulars of these agreements show their benefits.

Free Trade Agreements Offer Many Significant Benefits

In the case of Colombia, the FTA will provide duty-free access for more than 75 percent of US agricultural goods and more than 80 percent of US consumer products—helping to increase two-way trade, which reached more than $28 billion last year [2010]. The FTA—which is expected to help the American economy grow by $2.5 billion and US exports by $1.1 billion—allows us to seal a mutually beneficial deal with the third largest economy in South America and one of our longest standing democratic allies in the region.

Panama offers a key strategic location for US exporters to sell their goods and also to move them throughout the hemisphere via the Panama Canal. With canal expansion slated for completion in 2014, US companies in the machinery, infrastructure, and services sectors are anxious to see the FTA carried out to boost sales, exports, and employment opportunities for American workers. The agreement will also pave the way for more trade between the two nations, which reached $6.1 billion in 2010.

Finally, the South Korea agreement represents the most economically significant trade deal that the US has embarked on since the North American Free Trade Agreement [NAFTA]. All told, the South Korea FTA is expected to increase US exports by $11 billion, spur economic growth by nearly $12 billion, and support at least 70,000 American jobs.

At a time when the world economy has been stagnant, South Korea's economic growth exceeded 6 percent last year, making it the world's 15th largest economy. Opposition to the deal from domestic automakers and beef producers has been handled in agreements reached by the US and South Korean governments, and the South Korea FTA now enjoys widespread support—from the United Auto Workers and the National Cattlemen's Beef Association to big business.

Congress Is Swayed by Public Opinion and Not Economics

The economic arguments in favor of the FTAs are clear, so why has it taken so long to build support for these agreements in Congress, which is scheduled to vote on them today [in October 2011]? The answer lies in public opinion and politics. Proponents see trade liberalization as a win-win policy, but more than two-thirds of Americans believe that FTAs cost the United States jobs, according to an NBC News/*Wall Street Journal* poll conducted in September 2010. And nobody follows polls closer than politicians.

Free Trade Reflects US Traditions and Benefits Americans

Americans should appreciate the benefits of free trade more than most people, for we inhabit the greatest free-trade zone in the world. Michigan manufactures cars; New York provides banking; Texas pumps oil and gas. The fifty states trade freely with one another and that helps them all enjoy great prosperity. Indeed, one reason why the United States did so much better economically than Europe for more than two centuries is that America had free movement of goods and services while the European countries "protected" themselves from their neighbors. To appreciate the magnitudes involved, try to imagine how much your personal standard of living would suffer if you were not allowed to buy any goods or services that originated outside your home state.

A slogan occasionally seen on bumper stickers argues, "Buy American, save your job." This is grossly misleading for two main reasons. First, the costs of *saving* jobs in this particular way are enormous. Second, it is doubtful that any jobs are actually saved in the long run.

Alan S. Blinder, "Free Trade,"
The Concise Encyclopedia of Economics, *2008.*
www.econlib.org. Copyright © 2008 by Alan S. Blinder.

The reason for the public's skepticism lies in human nature. People like change in theory but it makes them nervous in fact, and trade accelerates change. Trade sharpens competition, forcing companies to move more quickly to gain advantage over their competitors. It propels US businesses to look outside our borders for new customers.

The United States is a mature, slow-growth economy, and it increasingly faces aggressive competition from overseas. When 95 percent of the world's consumers are also outside the US, anybody who wants to grow needs to look there, in addition to the domestic market.

More competition also means having to streamline production and increase productivity. For some companies, that has meant layoffs and movement of facilities offshore, which contributes to the unpopularity of trade. Indeed, the American manufacturing sector is greatly diminished.

But that's why the president has insisted on renewal of an expanded "Trade Adjustment Assistance" program as part of the FTA package, which will help displaced workers find new jobs. Historically we have not done that very well, but the expanded program will do a better job than before by providing workers an improved support structure (health benefits and relocation help). It also will extend unemployment compensation. Other measures to encourage US companies to stay here—such as corporate tax reform—would also help.

Regulations Are Included to Protect Against Unfair Practices

Another issue that contributes to public skepticism about trade is the unfair trade practices of other countries. The Senate has been debating Chinese practices—especially currency manipulation—for the past two weeks. Those are serious issues, and the administration has mounted an aggressive enforcement strategy using both World Trade Organization rules and America's own laws to combat them.

Fortunately, that is not as big of an issue with the new FTA countries. Having learned from the past, these agreements contain provisions, including ways to resolve disputes, that allow the parties to combat unfair practices if they turn up.

Congressional approval of the FTAs will not end the debate about trade, but it will increase jobs and help our economy grow—which are good things. Perhaps over time that growth will help Americans better understand that trade is an increasingly critical part of our economy that contributes to our prosperity.

"The majority of the jobs displaced would be in manufacturing, but many jobs would also be lost in industries that sell other goods and services to manufacturing."

Free Trade Leads to American Job Loss

Robert E. Scott

Robert E. Scott is an international economist for the Economic Policy Institute, with an expertise in international economics and trade agreements. In the following viewpoint, Scott examines proposed US trade agreements with Colombia and South Korea, and he projects that they are likely to increase the US trade deficit by $16.8 billion and eliminate or displace 214,000 American jobs. Scott notes that recent forecasts of the impacts of trade agreements on US trade deficits and employment have been highly flawed, and he reviews the factors that have contributed to these errors. Further, Scott concludes that contrary to the erroneous estimates from economists who say that the "Buy American" provisions in the American Recovery and Reinvestment Act of 2009 resulted in a net job loss, these provisions have actually saved US jobs while supporting the world's recovery from the global economic crisis.

As you read, consider the following questions:

1. According to the viewpoint, what was the increase in the average annual rate of growth of US imports from Mexico under NAFTA?

2. According to the author, in 2008, how many jobs could US imports from Colombia have supported if produced domestically?

3. How many jobs does Scott say have been saved or created by the American Recovery and Reinvestment Act of 2009?

The U.S. manufacturing sector lost 5.3 million jobs (nearly one-third of total employment) between January 2001 and September 2009. The United States accumulated a large, structural trade deficit over the past three decades, and in 2007, the non-oil share of this deficit was responsible for the loss or displacement of more than 5 million jobs. Although the U.S. trade deficit has fallen dramatically since July 2008, as a result of the worst recession in 70 years, many analysts project that the deficit will expand again once the recession ends.

This study examines proposed U.S. trade agreements with Colombia and South Korea and projects that they are likely to increase the U.S. trade deficit by $16.8 billion, and eliminate or displace 214,000 U.S. jobs. Other projections, which claim that these deals will create jobs in the United States, including those from the U.S. International Trade Commission and one published by the U.S. Chamber of Commerce, ignore factors such as the impact of trade deals on foreign direct investment (FDI) and the role played by exchange rate manipulation and most nontariff trade barriers, thereby underestimating the impact of these deals on U.S. imports and job losses.

The [2009] Chamber report also claims that "Buy American" provisions likely cost the United States nearly 200,000 jobs. This estimate ignores millions of jobs created by stimulus spending by the United States and other countries, and vastly overstates trade-related job displacement, by a factor of 30 or more.

This study examines the failed history of recent forecasts of the impacts of U.S. trade agreements, reviews the factors which have contributed to errors in the projections of the U.S. International Trade Commission and uses the lessons learned to analyze the Chamber report.

Economists Have a History of Failed Forecasts

Economists have been projecting that trade agreements between the United States and developing countries would generate an improving trade balance and support job creation in the United States for many years. These projections have usually been wrong. For example, [in 1993 Gary Clyde Hufbauer and Jeffrey J. Schott] projected U.S. exports to Mexico would rise more rapidly than imports following implementation of the North American Free Trade Agreement (NAFTA). In fact, the United States, which had a $1.7 billion trade surplus with Mexico in 1993, experienced a rapidly growing trade deficit that reached $74.8 billion in 2007, before declining to a $64.7 deficit in recession-influenced trade in 2008. Numerous other economists also predicted that NAFTA would generate rising trade surpluses that would support domestic job creation. Growing trade deficits with Mexico between 1993 and 2004 alone eliminated or displaced a net total of 560,000 U.S. jobs.

A particular source of concern is that the U.S. International Trade Commission (ITC), which generates official estimates of the likely impacts of proposed trade agreements, has generated many erroneous forecasts of the impacts of those agreements on U.S. trade, employment, and GDP [gross domestic product]. . . .

Free Trade Agreements Have Hurt American Trade and Jobs

Past projections by the ITC and many other economists regarding the outcomes of U.S. trade agreements have been erroneous, such as NAFTA and the agreement to provide China with permanent most favored nation (MFN) status (allowing it into the WTO [World Trade Organization]). There have also been flaws in the tariff-based economic models used by the ITC and the Chamber study, including the failure to include investment effects and the impacts of factors such as currency manipulation and nontariff barriers to trade. Given these problems, an alternative approach is clearly needed to assess the likely impacts of the proposed trade agreements with Colombia and South Korea on the U.S. economy. . . .

Under the NAFTA agreement, the average annual rate of growth of U.S. imports from Mexico accelerated from 12.7% per year to 19.1% per year, while the growth rate of U.S. exports to Mexico actually declined. This result is striking, because it stands at odds with projections by Hufbauer and Schott and many other economists that exports to Mexico would increase after NAFTA. Three factors explain this decline. First, there was a sharp rise in capital goods exports to Mexico in the pre-NAFTA period. [In 1997, Robert A.] Blecker noted that these exports supplied new export factories being built in Mexico to take advantage of the improved investment climate there, and the level of exports was unsustainable, given the buildup of Mexico's overall balance-of-payments deficit in this period. The 1994 peso crisis also resulted in a sharp fall in real incomes in Mexico (reducing demand for consumer goods from the United States) as well as a fall in the peso, which created an adverse shift in terms of trade for U.S.-made goods. There are striking similarities to Mexico in recent U.S. trade with Colombia. . . .

U.S. exports to and imports from China accelerated sharply following China's entry into the WTO. . . . Import growth increased 3.8 percentage points to 18.6% per year. Export growth nearly doubled, but from a tiny base. U.S. imports from China exceeded exports in 2001 by more than five to one, the United States' most imbalanced trade relationship. Despite the very high (20.2%) average annual rate of growth in exports to China in the 2001–08 period, this imbalance was largely unchanged (falling to 4.85:1 in 2008).

On average (of growth rates in U.S. trade with Mexico and Canada), ... U.S. import growth accelerated nearly twice as much as exports (import growth accelerated 5.1 percentage points while export growth accelerated only 2.8 percentage points). Furthermore, export growth accelerated in only one of two cases (China), and only from a very small base. Given China's reliance on the United States for feedstocks such as plastics, iron ore, and scrap, and for imported intermediates (such as electronic components), two outcomes were largely inevitable: that U.S. exports of these components would rise rapidly, and that the value of U.S. imports would rise even more rapidly since China was transforming imported inputs into valued manufactured final goods that were re-exported to the United States. . . .

The Projected Effects of Trade Agreements on U.S. Employment Reveal Significant Job Loss

Exports tend to support domestic employment, and imports displace production that could support domestic jobs. Most studies of the effects of proposed trade agreements begin by estimating the effects of those agreements on trade flows and then estimating the effects of changes in trade flows on domestic employment. [In 2008 Robert E.] Scott uses a 201 sector model of the economy and detailed data on trade flows in those industries to estimate the effects of changing trade patterns on employment.

In 2008, U.S. imports from Colombia could have supported 127,000 jobs if produced domestically, and exports supported 99,000 jobs, so net trade with Colombia resulted in a net displacement of 27,000 U.S. jobs. Given projected changes, the growth of the U.S. trade deficit with Colombia will displace 83,000 U.S. jobs in 2015, for a net loss of an additional 55,000 jobs. Likewise, the projected growth of U.S. trade deficits with Korea between 2008 and 2015 will displace an additional 159,000 U.S. jobs. Overall, if adopted, the U.S.-Colombia and U.S.-Korea trade agreements will displace a total of 214,000 additional U.S. jobs. The majority of the jobs displaced would be in manufacturing, but many jobs would also be lost in industries that sell other goods and services to manufacturing.

The Chamber study assumes that these trade agreements would lead to net increases in U.S. exports of $40 billion, and the creation of 383,400 jobs. This study has shown that the U.S. trade deficits with Colombia and Korea are instead likely to increase U.S. trade deficits with both countries by roughly $17 billion, resulting in the net loss of approximately 214,000 jobs.

The "Buy American" Provisions in the Recovery Act Save Jobs

The Chamber report also claims that inclusion of "Buy American" provisions in the American Recovery and Reinvestment Act of 2009 [referred to herein as the Recovery Act] could cause a net loss of 176,800 jobs if other countries retaliate with their own "Buy National" policies. This estimate is based on the observation that at least 90 countries or regions have announced stimulus plans totaling over $1.7 trillion. [In their 2009 report for the U.S. Chamber of Commerce, Laura M. Baughman and Joseph F. Francois] assume that 1% of this total is reserved for "Buy National" programs that reduce potential U.S. exports by approximately $17 billion, resulting in the job loss projections noted above.

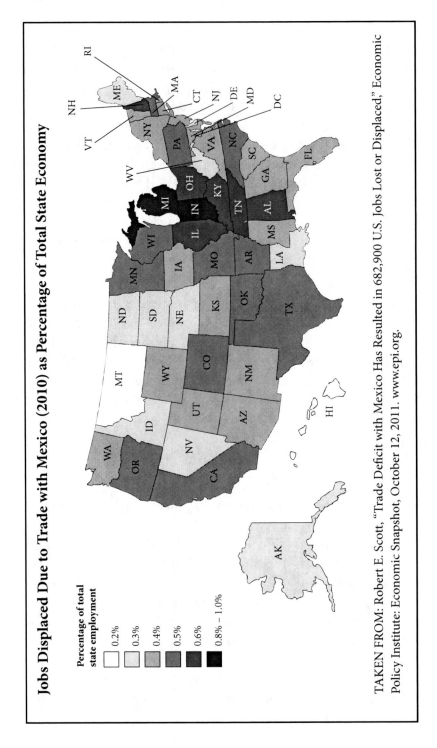

Jobs Displaced Due to Trade with Mexico (2010) as Percentage of Total State Economy

TAKEN FROM: Robert E. Scott, "Trade Deficit with Mexico Has Resulted in 682,900 U.S. Jobs Lost or Displaced," Economic Policy Institute: Economic Snapshot, October 12, 2011. www.epi.org.

This scenario is ludicrous for several reasons. First, as Paul Krugman pointed out in a recent [February 1, 2009] blog posting,

> We are in the midst of a global slump, with governments everywhere having trouble coming up with an effective response.... If macro policy isn't coordinated internationally—and it isn't—we'll tend to end up with too little fiscal stimulus everywhere.
>
> Now ask, how would this change if each country adopted protectionist measures that "contained" the effects of fiscal expansion with its domestic economy? Then everyone would adopt a more expansionary policy—and the world would get closer to full employment than it would otherwise. Yes, trade would be distorted, which is a cost; but the distortion caused by a severely underemployed world economy would be reduced. And, as the late [American economist] James Tobin liked to say, it takes a lot of Harberger triangles to fill an Okun gap.

In December 2009, the recession cost the United States some 10.6 million jobs. It is estimated that the Recovery Act has saved or created between 1 and 1.5 million jobs. Stimulus spending in other countries has accelerated the recovery of those economies, which will also be good for the U.S. economy.

The risks and potential costs of trade diversion cited by Baughman and Francois are vastly overstated, for at least two reasons. First, the Recovery Act contained explicit language that permits governments to waive the "Buy American" rules when they conflict with our international commitments under trade agreements such as NAFTA and the WTO. Second, the amount of U.S. trade potentially affected by "Buy National" rules is vastly overstated because other nations also have similar, reciprocal obligations to the United States. Most "Buy National" rules, including those in the United States, apply primarily to imports from countries like China and India that have not signed on to WTO or other government procurement codes.

Baughman and Francois estimate that only $3.2 billion of the $787 billion in Recovery Act spending (0.41%) will be affected by "Buy American" rules. If a similar proportion of the $1.7 trillion in stimulus spending by other countries (identified by Baughman and Francois) is affected by "Buy National" rules, then total *world* exports would decline by only $6.9 billion. However, the U.S. share of total world exports was only 8.1% in 2008. Thus, the U.S. share of "lost" exports would be on the order of one-half billion dollars. Baughman and Francois' estimate of the potential impact of "Buy National" rules is too large by a factor of 30.

But the more important point remains that the cost of "Buy National" policies pales in comparison with the benefits to be gained from more than $2.5 trillion in global stimulus spending, which will save or create millions of jobs worldwide. As Krugman notes, if building the political support needed to implement this spending diverts a few billion, or even tens of billions of dollars from world trade, the costs (in terms of jobs lost) are vastly outweighed by the benefits (in jobs saved or created) of increased stimulus spending needed to offset the worst global recession in 70 years.

VIEWPOINT 3

> *"Free trade is essential to America's continued prosperity. As the world's leading producer of goods and services, the United States needs to ensure that production and supply chains remain open in both directions."*

Removing Barriers to Trade Is Essential to a Sustained American Economic Recovery

Daniel J. Ikenson and Scott Lincicome

Daniel J. Ikenson is associate director of the Center for Trade Policy Studies at the Cato Institute. Scott Lincicome is an international trade attorney with the law firm of White & Case LLP, in Washington, DC. In the following viewpoint, Ikenson and Lincicome discuss the reasons why Americans tend to voice only tepid support for free trade agreements, and how experts in the government and the private sector can help to reshape the dialogue about and support for free trade, both in the United States and abroad. Free trade is essential to America's prosperity, the authors argue, and Americans must begin to realize that. They conclude that free trade is not only morally right because it ben-

efits all concerned parties, but also it is supportive of all political ideologies and the American economy because it gives US consumers greater choices and purchasing power and creates American jobs.

As you read, consider the following questions:

1. According to the viewpoint, what is the most principled case in support of free trade?

2. What do the authors say would be the result of limiting Americans' access to imports?

3. In what way do Ikenson and Lincicome see free trade as fair trade?

The 112th Congress begins its term [in 2011] amid renewed optimism about prospects for U.S. trade liberalization. Big labor's stranglehold over the congressional trade agenda was broken with the election in November. The U.S. government finally appears willing to end its disgraceful ban on Mexican trucks. And in his State of the Union address, President [Barack] Obama implored Congress to pass the trade agreement with South Korea as soon as possible, and articulated his commitment to bringing the other two pending bilateral agreements, as well as the Trans-Pacific Partnership negotiations and the Doha Round, to successful conclusions.

After four years of stasis on the trade front, the new environment is a welcome change. Removing barriers to trade—in both directions—is essential to sustained economic recovery and long-term growth.

But how long will this window of opportunity remain ajar? Despite trade's benefits, American sentiment toward it is lukewarm in the best of times, and always vulnerable to manipulation by politicians and media charlatans looking to blame foreigners for domestic shortcomings. Before the end of this year, the 2012 presidential election campaigns will be in high gear—and trade has been a particularly dirty word in stump speeches and political debates in the past. Indeed, one of the reasons for the energetic trade policy push in 2011 is that the political environment next year is expected to be less hospitable to trade initiatives.

The fact that public opinion about trade is so malleable and arguments for restricting it so resonant at times speaks to a failure of free trade's proponents to make their compelling message stick. It is sad but true that so many Americans need to be reminded of the benefits of being free to choose how and with whom to conduct commerce. But in an atmosphere where demagogues peddle myths to mislead the public into believing that it is preferable for government to limit their choices and direct their resources to chosen ends, it is crucial that the case for free trade be made more clearly, comprehensively, and consistently than it has been in the past. . . .

Some of the most compelling arguments for free trade have been only modestly summoned or absent from the discussion for too long.

The Message Matters When It Comes to Support for Free Trade

Most Americans enjoy the fruits of international trade and globalization every day: driving to work in vehicles containing at least some foreign content, relying on smart phones assembled abroad from parts made in multiple countries (including the United States), having more to save or spend because retailers pass on cost savings made possible by their access to thousands of foreign producers, designing and selling products that would never have been commercially viable without access to the cost efficiencies afforded by transnational production and supply chains, enjoying fresh imported produce that was once unavailable out of season, depositing bigger paychecks on account of their employers' growing sales to customers abroad, and enjoying salaries and benefits provided by employers that happen to be foreign-owned companies.

Nevertheless, public opinion polls routinely find tepid support among Americans for free trade. Regardless of the prevailing economic conditions; how the questions are phrased; or whether the subject is attitudes toward free trade, trade agreements, or the impact of trade on the U.S. economy, most polls typically find that fewer than half of all Americans view trade favorably and that skeptical views have become more prevalent in recent years.

Some of that skepticism can be attributed to the perpetuation of myths about how unfair foreign trade practices have destroyed the U.S. manufacturing sector or about how the trade deficit reflects a failure of trade policy and constitutes a drag on economic growth—the staple arguments of most protectionists. However, we free trade advocates need to bear some of the responsibility for not winning Americans' hearts and minds. . . .

The poll data make clear that better salesmanship—or a better strategy—could change minds. . . . A significant segment of the population—at least 10 percent—changes its views on trade fairly regularly. Given that most Americans have not lost their jobs to import competition or outsourcing, nor do very many Americans know someone who has, it seems unlikely that deteriorating attitudes toward trade have much, if anything, to do with personal experience. . . . American attitudes toward trade are shaped largely by what Americans hear from their elected officials and what they absorb from the media.

The dramatic decline in pro-trade sentiment between 2007 and 2008 coincided with a U.S. presidential primary election campaign season in which the Democratic candidates routinely criticized U.S. trade policy and certain trade partners. . . .

The fairly significant increase in pro-trade sentiment during 2009 was likely attributable in part to the fact that a very public disavowal of protectionism took place on the international stage, as governments grappled with alternative policies to combat the recession. . . .

Furthermore, in early 2009, President Obama visited heads of state in Canada and Mexico, offering reassurances that his campaign pledge to reopen NAFTA [North American Free Trade Agreement] may have been a bit too hasty. And his instructions to Congress, at about the same time, that emerging "Buy American" provisions should not violate U.S. trade commitments, signaled to the public that the president might be less hostile to trade than he appeared to be during the previous year. The president's first trade policy agenda . . . revealed an administration far more approving than skeptical of free trade. . . .

The subsequent decline in public support between 2009 and 2010 might have had something to do with rising tensions in the U.S.-China trade relationship, which was covered intensively—perhaps even incited—by the media, and which spawned numerous congressional hearings into various Chinese policies and practices and a Democratic Party 2010 campaign strategy—"Make It in America"—that placed much of the blame for America's alleged manufacturing decline squarely on China. Also, during this period, President Obama frequently asserted that China's "undervalued currency" was to blame for the U.S.-China trade deficit. . . .

The Stock Pro-Trade Message Contains the Seeds of Its Own Destruction

It is fair to say that trade skeptics have the upper hand in the battle over messaging. . . .

One explanation for the resonance of anti-trade sentiment is that it is easier to whip up public opinion by playing to stereotypes and characterizing trade as a zero-sum game between "us" (Americans) and "them" (foreigners) than it is to explain the process by which economic value is created and how free trade facilitates that process. Theirs is a black-and-white message. Once the public's mind has been filled with images of shuttered factories and unemployed workers—regardless of the real cause of those conditions—it becomes more difficult to convey the truth about how Americans benefit from trade and how much poorer we would be without it.

But that hurdle can be overcome. The solution requires more than rationalization; it requires introspection, then change. Many of trade's most vocal and active proponents in government and the private sector have relied too heavily and for too long on a faulty marketing strategy, which posits that more trade and more trade agreements mean more export opportunities, and more exports mean more economic growth and more jobs. . . .

However, that message invites the following retort: If exports help grow the economy and create jobs, then imports must shrink the economy and cost jobs. In failing to explain why that conclusion about imports is wrong, trade proponents have yielded the floor to trade skeptics, who have been more than happy to manufacture talking points about the "deleterious" impact of imports on the U.S. economy. Most of those talking points are misleading or plain wrong, but there has been inadequate effort to correct the record. . . .

The pervasive view that exports are good and imports are bad is a central misconception upon which rests the belief that trade negotiations and "reciprocity" are essential to trade liberalization. . . . This misguided premise that imports are the cost of exports and should be minimized lies at the root of public skepticism about trade. Ironically, it is also a prominent feature of the favored pro-trade argument. . . .

In his State of the Union speech, President Obama referred to his administration's goal of doubling exports by 2014—a goal for which an entire bureaucracy has been erected—to make the point that "the more we export, the more jobs we create at home." Not once in that speech did the president acknowledge the importance of imports to the bottom lines of those U.S. companies that he expects to create American jobs. The problem is not that export potential is used as a selling point. The problem is that it is too often the exclusive selling point, and that contributes to unfavorable impressions about imports and the trade deficit—two statistics, by the way, that typically increase when the economy is expanding and fall when the economy is contracting. . . .

Of the "Top Ten Reasons Trade Is Good for America," a list extracted from a recent letter to Congress from a coalition of businesses and posted on the website of the U.S. Chamber of Commerce, only one made reference to imports. . . . We must articulate a more resonant message so that the benefits of trade need not be rationalized or couched in defensive rhetoric.

A More Compelling Case for Free Trade Must Be Made

The case for free trade is much broader than the one that trumpets only export potential. And it is more elegant. The most principled case is a moral one: Voluntary economic exchange is inherently fair, benefits both parties, and allocates scarce resources more efficiently than a system under which government dictates or limits choices. Moreover, government intervention in voluntary economic exchange on behalf of some citizens necessarily comes at the expense of others and is inherently unfair, inefficient, and subverts the rule of law. At their core, trade barriers are the triumph of coercion and politics over free choice and economics. Trade barriers are the result of productive resources being diverted to achieve political ends and, in the process, taxing unsuspecting consumers to line the pockets of the special interests that succeeded in enlisting the weight of the government on their side.

Protectionism is akin to earmarks, but it comes out of the hides of American families and businesses instead of the general treasury. Policy makers on the right should support free trade because it is consistent with their principled opposition to higher taxes on American businesses and consumers and to big government telling people how and where they should spend their money. A vote for free trade is a vote to cut taxes and to get government out of the business of picking winners and losers in the market. Policy makers on the left should support free trade because it is consistent with their opposition to corporate welfare and regressive taxation.

Beyond the moral case for free trade, when people are free to buy from, sell to, and invest with one another as they choose, they can achieve far more than when governments attempt to control their decisions. . . . Free markets are essential to prosperity, and expanding free markets as much as possible enhances that prosperity.

When goods, services, and capital flow freely across U.S. borders, Americans can take full advantage of the opportunities of the international marketplace. . . . Study after study has shown that countries that are more open to the global economy grow faster and achieve higher incomes than those that are relatively closed.

Common Myths Must Be Refuted

In the bright light of these broader free trade arguments, it becomes clear that those seeking to restrict trade are trying to commit an offense. They are attempting to enlist the force of government—via higher taxes, more regulation, or corporate welfare—to prevent individuals from engaging in consensual, mutually beneficial exchange. And they should be forced to explain themselves in terms of the harm they would inflict on others through state coercion. Regrettably, that never happens.

Instead, those seeking protection claim immunity from the logic and equity of those moral and economic parameters,

Low Trade Barriers Reduce Unemployment and Poverty

Special interest groups often complain that "unfair" foreign competition destroys jobs, but countries with the highest trade barriers have nearly twice the unemployment rate of countries with the most trade freedom. In the United States, the trade deficit and the unemployment rate usually have an inverse relationship. When the trade deficit increases, the unemployment rate decreases, and vice versa. For example, in 2009, the U.S. trade deficit shrank by 46 percent, and the unemployment rate increased by 60 percent.

Many critics of trade deals, such as the North American Free Trade Agreement (NAFTA) and the WTO [World Trade Organization] agreement, argue that free trade benefits big multinational corporations and "the rich" at the expense of everyone else. In fact, . . . poverty rates are lower in countries with low trade barriers.

Bryan Riley and Ambassador Terry Miller,
"Global Trade Freedom Needs a Boost," Heritage Foundation,
October 7, 2011. www.heritage.org.

preferring to invoke claims of exceptional circumstances, labeling those opposed to their agenda as unpatriotic, or playing on fears about the consequences of exercising one's rights to trade. Of course free trade is ideal in theory, they will say, but reality demands special consideration in our case. Or, of course individuals should be free to choose with whom they transact, but their expressed preferences for imports imperil their jobs and America's future.

Trade skepticism is rooted in fear, which thrives on the propagation and acceptance of recycled myths. . . .

The allegation that imports have destroyed the U.S. manu-facturing sector persists despite the wealth of evidence to the contrary. U.S. manufacturing took its lumps during the recent recession (as did all other sectors of the economy), but by all credible metrics it has been thriving for decades. In fact, U.S. factories account for more value-added manufacturing than the factories of any other country in the world.

If imports detract from growth and reduce the number of jobs in the economy, then why does import value tend to rise when the economy is expanding and adding jobs and fall when the economy is contracting and shedding jobs? Imports are vital to economic growth. . . .

By limiting Americans' access to imports, production costs and other business costs would be higher, necessitating higher prices, lower wages, and other cost savings to make enterprises profitable. Consumers, businesses, and government would have less purchasing power, which would curtail economic growth and hurt U.S. companies trying to compete abroad, thus reducing exports. In fact, export sales would be even more difficult to come by, as foreigners, deprived of their sales to Americans, would have fewer dollars to spend on U.S. goods.

Contrary to some assertions, imports actually support jobs in U.S. manufacturing and in many other sectors of the economy. In addition to the imported intermediate goods that keep U.S. companies competitive and able to provide jobs, a significant percentage of U.S. imports are final goods that were simply assembled abroad from components produced, designs engineered, and ideas hatched in the United States. Without access to lower-cost labor in places like China, prod-ucts like Apple's iPod, iPhone, and iPad might never have been commercially viable. . . .

The example of the iPhone production and supply chain also reveals the absurdity of hand-wringing over trade deficits. The alleged U.S. high-tech trade deficit with China is simply a function of antiquated trade flow accounting that has failed to keep up with the reality of globalization. Even though each iPhone imported from China registers as a $179 import (the full cost of its production), only $6.50 of that amount represents the cost of Chinese inputs. The bottom line is that each iPhone imported from China supports U.S. employment up and down the supply chain, from Apple's designers and engineers to independent component manufacturers to logistics providers, truckers, port workers, and retail employees. . . .

Five Benefits of Free Trade for Americans

In order to win the hearts and minds of a skeptical American public, trade advocates need to broaden their arguments to include more than just happy talk about potential export growth. The case for free trade is more compelling than that. In light of the arguments above, we conclude with the five most compelling reasons free trade is good for America.

1. Free trade is fair trade. Trade occurs between individuals, not countries. This voluntary economic exchange is inherently fair, benefits both parties, and allocates scarce resources more efficiently than a system under which government dictates or limits choices. It is thus morally imperative that Americans have the freedom to engage in commerce with whomever they choose.

2. Free trade is appealing across the political spectrum. Free trade is consistent with the imperative of smaller government (lower taxes and fewer restrictions), greater transparency (fewer backroom deals—think Mexican truck ban), opposition to corporate welfare, and opposition to regressive taxation.

3. Free trade is just the extension of free markets across national borders. Widening the circle of people with whom we transact brings benefits to consumers in the form of lower prices, greater variety, and better quality,

and it allows companies to reap the benefits of innovation, specialization, and economies of scale that larger markets afford. Free markets are essential to prosperity, and expanding free markets as much as possible enhances that prosperity.

4. Free trade creates prosperity and supports rising living standards. Study after study has shown that countries that are more open to the global economy grow faster and achieve higher incomes than those that are relatively closed. When goods, services, and capital flow freely across U.S. borders, Americans can take full advantage of the opportunities of the international marketplace. They can buy the best or least expensive goods and services the world has to offer; they can sell to the most promising markets; they can choose among the best investment opportunities; and they can tap into the worldwide pool of labor and capital.

5. Free trade is essential to America's continued prosperity. As the world's leading producer of goods and services, the United States needs to ensure that production and supply chains remain open in both directions so that foreigners can sell intermediate goods to U.S. producers and final goods to U.S. consumers, and so they can earn U.S. dollars with which they can consume U.S. products and services and invest in the United States.

"*The present international trading order will not be here in ten years, and quite likely not in five. The unsustainable American trade deficit alone makes this a certainty.*"

Trade Restrictions Protect American Workers and Help Restore the US Economy

Ian Fletcher

Ian Fletcher is a senior economist at the San Francisco office of the Coalition for a Prosperous America. In the following viewpoint, Fletcher contends that the current US free trade policy is responsible for killing American jobs, primarily because the US trade deficit continues to act as a giant "reverse stimulus" to the American economy. Fletcher asserts that the American economy does not create jobs in growing fields like technology or green energy because these jobs are being exported and the purported benefits of free trade do not exist. Fletcher refutes many arguments in favor of free trade and recommends the implementation of restrictions on trade to protect American jobs, as was done successfully in the past.

As you read, consider the following questions:

1. According to Fletcher, what has the US trade deficit been for the past decade (in billions of dollars per year)?

2. As stated in the viewpoint, what is the myth that David Ricardo's theory of 1817 seems to support?

3. What idea of Kevin Kearns does Fletcher support in this viewpoint?

One thing is for certain already: The present international trading order will not be here in ten years, and quite likely not in five. The unsustainable American trade deficit alone makes this a certainty.

Since the end of the Cold War, and accelerating after NAFTA [North American Free Trade Agreement] in 1994, that order has consisted in ever-expanding "free" trade worldwide—which in reality is a curious mixture of genuinely free trade practiced by the United States and a few others with the technocratic mercantilism of surging East Asia and Germanic-Scandinavian Europe.

From America's point of view, this order is free trade, at least on the import side of the equation, so it is as free trade that we must criticize it, prepare to celebrate its passing, and investigate what should replace it.

Our free trade policy is the answer to a question that currently has most mainstream economists scratching their heads: *What killed the great American job machine?* This policy has been partly responsible for increasing inequality in the United States and the gradual repudiation of our 200-year tradition of broadly shared middle-class prosperity. It is a major player in our rising indebtedness, community abandonment, and a weakening of the industrial sinews of our national security.

America's economy today continues to struggle to emerge from recession because our trade deficit—fluctuating around $500 billion a year for a decade now—acts as a giant "reverse stimulus" to our economy. It causes a huge slice of domestic demand to flow not into domestic jobs, thus domestic wages and thus more demand, but into imports, therefore foreign wages, and therefore a boom in Guangdong, China; Seoul, South Korea; Yokohama, Japan; and even Munich—not Gary, Indiana; Fontana, California; and the other badlands of America's industrial decline. Our response? Yet more stimulus, leading to an ever-increasing overhang of debt, both foreign and domestic, the cost of whose servicing then exerts its own drag on recovery.

The American economy has, in fact, entirely lost the ability to create jobs in tradable sectors. This cheery fact comes straight from the Commerce Department. *All* our net new jobs are in non-tradable services: a few heart surgeons and a legion of bus boys and security guards, most of them without health insurance or retirement benefits. These are dead-end jobs, and our economy as a whole is also being similarly squeezed into dead-end industries. The green jobs of the future? Gone to places like China where governments bid sweeter subsidies than Massachusetts can afford. Nanotechnology? Perhaps the first major technology in a century where America is not the leading innovator. Foreign subsidies are illegal under WTO [World Trade Organization] rules, but no matter: Who's going to enforce them when corporate America is happily lapping at their very trough?

The Benefits of Free Trade Are a Myth

All the complaints just mentioned are familiar to the public, but they fly in the face of a sanctified myth that the superiority of free trade is a known truth of social science. Supposedly, it was proved long ago that protectionism is just a racket for the benefit of special interests at the expense of consumers.

Never mind that every developed nation, from England to South Korea, and including the United States, *became* a developed nation by means of this policy. That little piece of economic history is airbrushed out of the picture in favor of the Cold War myth of the absolute superiority of perfectly free markets. America never embraced this myth on its merits, merely as a tactical device to prop up the noncommunist economies of the world and make them dependent upon us.

The cycle repeats: China today is reenacting this 400-year-old mercantilist playbook, which was born among the city-states of Renaissance Italy and never quite forgotten.

Economic theory will be sorted out eventually. Thanks to the work of a small, brave group of dissident economists—scholars like Ralph Gomory, William Baumol, Erik Reinert, and Ha-Joon Chang—the credibility of free trade as a theoretical doctrine is crumbling, and the discipline will eventually change its mind. But it will almost certainly be a lagging indicator, ready to vindicate policy forged in crisis well after the dust has settled. Academia is a superb rationalizer, and will doubtless find a way to avoid embarrassing questions about its own past positions when it teaches undergraduates twenty years from now that free trade is a delusion and a mistake.

The Problems with Free Trade Are Numerous

What's wrong with free trade? A whole host of problems, many of them long known to economists but assumed in recent decades to be unimportant.

The technical plot thickens here fast, but we can begin by noting that any serious discussion of free trade must confront David Ricardo's celebrated 1817 theory of comparative advantage, whose tale of English cloth and Portuguese wine is familiar to generations of economics students. According to a myth accepted by both laypeople and far too many professional economists, this theory proves that free trade is best, always and everywhere, regardless of whether a nation's trading partners reciprocate.

Unfortunately for free traders, this theory is riddled with dubious assumptions, some of which even Ricardo acknowledged. If they held true, the hypothesis would hold water. But because they often don't, it is largely inapplicable in the real world. Here's why:

Ricardo's first dubious assumption is that trade is sustainable. But when a nation imports so much that it runs a trade deficit, this means it is either selling assets to foreign nations or going into debt to them. These processes, while elastic, aren't infinitely so. This is precisely the situation the United States is in today: Not only does it risk an eventual crash, but in the meantime, every dollar of assets it sells and every dollar of debt it assumes reduces the nation's net worth.

Ricardo's second dubious assumption is that the productive assets used to generate goods and services can easily be shifted from declining to rising industries. But laid-off autoworkers and abandoned automobile plants don't generally transition easily to making helicopters. Assistance payments can blunt the pain, but these costs must be counted against the purported benefits of free trade, and they make free trade an enlarger of big government.

The third dubious assumption is that free trade doesn't worsen income inequality. But, in reality, it squeezes the wages of ordinary Americans because it expands the world's effective supply of labor, which can move from rice paddy to factory overnight, faster than its supply of capital, which takes decades to accumulate at prevailing savings rates. As a result, free trade strengthens the bargaining position of capital relative to labor. And there is no guarantee that ordinary people's gains from cheaper imports will outweigh their losses from lowered wages.

The fourth dubious assumption is that capital isn't internationally mobile. If it can't move between nations, then free trade will (if the other assumptions hold true) steer it to the most productive use in our own economy. But if capital can move between nations, then free trade may reveal that it can be used better somewhere else. This will benefit the nation that the capital migrates to, and the world economy as a whole, but it won't always benefit us.

The fifth dubious assumption is that free trade won't turn benign trading partners into dangerous trading rivals. But free trade often does do this, as we see today in China, whose growth is massively dependent upon exports. This is especially likely when trading partners practice mercantilism, the 400-year-old strategy of deliberately gaming the world trading system by methods like currency manipulation and hidden tariffs.

The sixth dubious assumption is that short-term efficiency leads to long-term growth. But such growth has more to do with creative destruction, innovation, and capital accumulation than it does with short-term efficiency. All developed nations, including the United States, industrialized by means of protectionist policies that were inefficient in the short run.

What is the implication of all these loopholes in Ricardo's theory? That trade is good for America, but free trade, which is not the same thing at all, is a very dicey proposition.

A New Way of Thinking About Trade Is Emerging

Beyond the holes in [Ricardo's theory], there is an entirely new way of looking at trade growing up around the theoretical insights of Ralph Gomory and William Baumol of New York University. The details are technical, but the upshot is they have managed to bridge the gap between the Pollyannaish "international trade is always win-win" Ricardian view and the overly pessimistic "international trade is war" view. The former view is naive; the latter ignores the fact that economics precisely *isn't* war because it is a positive-sum game in which goods are produced, not just divided, making mutual gains possible.

Why Globalization Has Not Helped American Workers

Globalization is dramatically disconnecting the relationship between American corporate employers and their employees. There has always been conflict over the shares of the benefits of worker productivity going to profits and wages. But until recently, you could assume that both workers and businesses had a common interest in producing in America. . . .

We are no longer just talking about simple trade among economies defined by national frontiers. Today's globalization represents the creation of a world market without the enforceable rules that make markets work for everyone's benefit. Led by multinational corporate interests, American policy makers pushed American workers into a brutally competitive market that resembles not so much the future, but the past: the 19th-century dog-eat-dog robber baron [American capitalists who became wealthy through exploitation] era.

Jeff Faux and Andrea Orr,
"Trade Policy and the American Worker,"
Economic Policy Institute, May 3, 2010. www.epi.org.

So at long last, someone has given us a theoretical framework that can accommodate economic reality as we actually experience it, not just lecture us on what "must" happen as Ricardianism does. It's both a dog-eat-dog *and* a scratch-my-back-and-I'll-scratch-yours world. *Economics has finally given common sense permission to be true.* Ironically, their sophisticated mathematical models are actually closer to the thinking of the man on the street than those they replaced.

Trade Restrictions Are Crucial and Warranted

There is an appropriate policy response. For starters, the United States should apply compensatory tariffs against imports subsidized by currency manipulation, an idea that originated with Kevin Kearns of the U.S. Business and Industry Council and was passed by the House of Representatives in the previous Congress. Also essential is a border tax to counter foreign export rebates implemented by means of foreign value-added taxes.

Perhaps even more important than the pure economics of free trade is its *political economy* (an older and more accurate term). For the fundamental reality of free trade is that it relieves corporate America from any substantial economic tie to the economic well-being of ordinary Americans. If corporate America can produce its products anywhere, and sell them anywhere, then it has no incentive to care about the capacity of Americans to produce or consume. Conversely, if it is tied to making a profit by selling goods made *by* Americans *to* Americans, then it has a natural incentive to care about American productivity and consumption.

Productivity and consumption *are* prosperity. The rest is details.

Right now, America is confronting any number of long- and short-term economic problems with one hand tied behind its back: Corporate America is, increasingly, quietly indifferent to America's economic success. This must change. While any proposals to end the K Street dictatorship in America's public life are welcome, the reality is that mechanical reforms are less likely to touch on true fundamentals than realigning the economic incentives they reflect.

This is not a utopian project. In fact, it has already been accomplished, during the long 1790–1945 era of American protectionism. America wandered away from Founding Father Alexander Hamilton's vision of a relatively self-contained

American economy in order to win the Cold War. We threw our markets open to the world as a bribe not to go Communist. If we fail to return to a policy of strategic, not unconditional, economic openness, we may lose the next Cold War—to a Confucian authoritarianism no less opposed to the idea of a free society than Marxism, and considerably more efficient.

> *"Advanced manufacturing policy ... is about strengthening a sector that is a key catalyst of employment and economic growth. And it's about ensuring the international competitiveness of the US economy [and] closing the trade deficit."*

Incentives for American Manufacturers Boost US Prosperity and Global Trade Competitiveness

Devon Swezey

Devon Swezey is project director for the Breakthrough Institute, where he works as an energy and climate policy analyst. In the following viewpoint, Swezey explains why a healthy domestic manufacturing sector is essential to America's prosperity in the twenty-first century, stating that investment in new product and process innovations is what drives economic growth in the long term and that manufacturing is absolutely central to innovation. Swezey concludes that in addition to its many other benefits, manufacturing in the United States helps to lower trade deficits, which will in turn create jobs.

Devon Swezey, "Romer Misses the Mark on Manufacturing," The Breakthrough Institute, February 9, 2012. www.thebreakthrough.org. Copyright © 2012 by The Breakthrough Institute. All rights reserved. Reproduced by permission.

As you read, consider the following questions:

1. What percentage of US scientists and engineers does Swezey contend are employed by the nation's investment in research and development?

2. What does the viewpoint state is a likely outcome of losing high-tech manufacturing?

3. What does Swezey say is the percentage of US exports composed of manufactured goods?

A healthy manufacturing sector is essential to America's economic prosperity in the 21st century. But you wouldn't know that reading last Sunday's [February 4, 2012] New York Times, where former [Barack] Obama administration Council of Economic Advisors [CEA] chair Christina Romer writes that there are no compelling reasons for US manufacturing policy.

According to Romer, the recent hubbub about manufacturing is due to the fact that people have a "feeling" that "making things" is important. In reality, she writes, consumers "value haircuts as much as hair dryers." To be sure, all of us need haircuts, some of us more than others. But Romer's argument that we should value all industries of the economy the same is just not true. It's reminiscent of economist Michael Boskin, another former CEA chair, who said it doesn't matter whether a country makes computer chips or potato chips.

The fact is that some industries are characterized by high productivity and economies of scale that reduce costs and drive economic growth throughout the economy. As Clyde Prestowitz writes of Romer's own example:

Production of hair dryers can be done in large factories that produce economies of scale. Such scale economies lead to lower prices, lower inflation, higher productivity and thus higher wealth creation for the whole economy. In addition, producers of hair dryers invest in research and development to foster innovation of new, more efficient, less energy using, and easier to produce dryers.

Driving Economic Growth by Investing in Manufacturing

Investment in new product and process innovations is what drives economic growth over the long term. And . . . manufacturing is absolutely central to innovation, something that many economists like Romer and economic commentators like Matt Yglesias don't seem to understand. The manufacturing sector comprises two-thirds of the nation's industry investment in research and development (R&D) and employs nearly 64% of the country's scientists and engineers.

But Romer doesn't mention manufacturing's importance to innovation in her article. Instead, she prefers to argue with what she sees as the common rationales for manufacturing policy—market failures, jobs, and inequality—none of which she finds "completely convincing."

On the first issue, she writes that market failures in manufacturing—where positive spillovers mean that some benefits of a new manufacturing plant go to other companies in the area, thus providing a rationale for government investment—are small, citing two academic studies on the subject. But many other studies have found that manufacturing is a central component of regional industrial ecosystems, and that being near manufacturing can accelerate innovation and strengthen regional competitiveness. As President [George W.] Bush's Council of Advisors on Science and Technology wrote in 2004, "design, product development, and process evolution all benefit from proximity to manufacturing, so that new ideas can be tested and discussed with those 'working on the ground.'"

Indeed, recent research suggests that losing high-tech manufacturing can imperil a nation's capacity for future innovation. Harvard's Gary Pisano and Willy Shih write that

America's "industrial commons"—the collective engineering, R&D and manufacturing capabilities that sustain innovation—are being hollowed out and the United States can no longer produce many high-tech products. Moreover, research and design are starting to follow high-tech manufacturing abroad, imperiling America's historic advantages in innovation.

Next, Romer writes that the impact of manufacturing on jobs relative to the employment needs of the economy is small and that we should focus on boosting aggregate demand instead:

> Unemployment today is high, but not because of a decline in manufacturing. That decline has been going on for 30 years—and for most of the 1990s and 2000s, the unemployment rate was less than 6 percent.

Put aside that this obscures the fact that manufacturing employment generally followed the business cycle with only modest declines until 2000 when it fell off a cliff—declining by 5.5 million jobs from 2000 to 2008, or 32 percent. Romer understates the impact of manufacturing on jobs for two key reasons.

Why Manufacturing Matters

First, she ignores the fact that manufacturing facilities have extensive backward linkages, generating output and employment throughout the economy. Indeed, manufacturing's "multiplier effect" in terms of both output and employment is larger than any other sector of the economy. Specifically, studies demonstrate that every dollar in final sales of manufactured products supports $1.40 in output from other sectors of the economy. And the average job in manufacturing produces two to three spin-off jobs elsewhere in the economy. Even if employment on the factory floor never reaches levels of previous decades, when these effects are taken into account, manufacturing's employment footprint is quite substantial.

What Manufacturing Means to the United States

Manufacturing matters to the United States because it provides high-wage jobs, commercial innovation (the nation's largest source), a key to trade deficit reduction, and a disproportionately large contribution to environmental sustainability. The manufacturing industries and firms that make the greatest contribution to these four objectives are also those that have the greatest potential to maintain or expand employment in the United States. Computers and electronics, chemicals (including pharmaceuticals), transportation equipment (including aerospace and motor vehicles and parts), and machinery are especially important....

American manufacturing will not realize its potential automatically. While U.S. manufacturing performs well compared to the rest of the U.S. economy, it performs poorly compared to manufacturing in other high-wage countries. American manufacturing needs strengthening in four key areas:

- Research and development.

- Lifelong training of workers at all levels.

- Improved access to finance.

- An increased role for workers and communities in creating and sharing in the gains from innovative manufacturing.

Susan Helper, Timothy Krueger, and Howard Wial, "Why Does Manufacturing Matter? Which Manufacturing Matters?: A Policy Framework," Brookings Institution Press, 2012. www.brookings.edu. Copyright © 2012 by Brookings Institution Press. All rights reserved. Reproduced by permission.

Second, Romer completely misses the connection between America's persistent, massive trade deficits and our employment situation. In 2010 the trade deficit stood at nearly $500 billion, down from a record of $760 billion in 2006. With such large deficits, it's difficult to see how more fiscal stimulus to boost aggregate demand, which Romer favors, will fill the jobs hole in the economy. It would certainly create some jobs, but much of that demand would be filled by imports, which creates jobs in other countries. Rather, eliminating the trade deficit would create millions of jobs in the United States.

Increasing Manufacturing Can Lower Trade Deficits

And the best way to close the trade deficit is by expanding manufactured exports. This is because the large majority of US trade—nearly 70% of exports and 83% of imports—is still in goods. Manufactured goods in particular comprise 57% of US exports. Can exporting services help reduce the trade deficit? Absolutely, and the United States enjoyed a $149 billion surplus in services in 2010. But it took 11 years for service exports to double to its 2010 level of $543 billion. The simple arithmetic shows that the current positive balance in services would need to quadruple to eliminate the deficit in goods. This is implausible, to say the least.

What about inequality? Romer writes correctly that while manufacturing pays higher-than-average wages, it is no longer a source of high-paying jobs for less educated workers. Manufacturing is a technologically sophisticated enterprise and today's manufacturing workers must have a wide array of abilities, including the production skills to set up and operate processes, design and development skills to continuously improve those processes, as well as proficiency in maintenance, repair and supply chain logistics. But then the policy response should not be to ignore manufacturing but ensure that workers have the skills for advanced manufacturing industries.

Romer ends by implying that manufacturing policy is driven by economic nostalgia for an earlier age, writing, "public policy needs to go beyond sentiment and history." To be sure, policy must account for the ways in which manufacturing has changed over previous decades. Some labor-intensive industries are likely gone for good, while the increasing use of information technology, robotics, and high-precision tools means that today's factory workers must have much greater skills than previous generations.

Fortunately, advanced manufacturing policy need not be about sentimentality or history, but about creating the next generation of advanced technologies that spur innovation, drive productivity, and power economic growth in the 21st century. It is about strengthening a sector that is a key catalyst of employment and economic growth. And it's about ensuring the international competitiveness of the US economy, closing the trade deficit and out-competing other nations whose governments rightly view high-tech manufacturing as a strategic industry.

The good news is that the Obama administration has recently recognized that advanced manufacturing is critical for the future prosperity of the US economy, even if its former chief economist does not.

"Action is necessary, but it should focus on preparing future generations to compete in a global marketplace, through education reform and retraining current workers who lose their jobs due to trade."

Protectionist Manufacturing Trade Policies Undermine American Competitiveness in the Global Marketplace

Matthew Jensen

Matthew Jensen is an economic researcher at the American Enterprise Institute for Public Policy Research. In the following viewpoint, Jensen discusses how the changes in the character of international trade over the last several decades have, in turn, changed where and how businesses operate. He contends that protectionist policies no longer have a place in development of trade and that such practices only hurt businesses and ruin the future of the US economy. When companies' options for trade, labor, or location are limited, Jensen asserts, they become less competitive, and this is bad for the economy in many ways, including jobs. Jensen adds that because the supply chains for busi-

nesses are now global rather than local, outmoded ideas for targeting specific regions or industries are no longer viable options for successful businesses. Furthermore, he concludes, the arbitrary nature of business clusters makes predictions unreliable.

As you read, consider the following questions:

1. According to the viewpoint, what are two changes that have allowed businesses to slice the production process into pieces?

2. Jensen states that a reality that once argued in favor of industrial subsidies is no longer a reality. What was that reality?

3. Why did Switzerland become the world's watch capital, according to Jensen?

Over the last several decades, the character of international trade has changed dramatically. Drastic advances in communication and information technologies have allowed businesses to slice the production process into pieces which are then located in their most efficient locations. Supply chains are formed that stretch across the globe, and individual parts, components, and even tasks, are traded from one country to another within these chains.

In his State of the Union address, President [Barack] Obama condemned this practice, saying, "It's time to stop rewarding businesses that ship jobs overseas, and start rewarding companies that create jobs right here in America." More specifically, he wants to conduct industrial targeting, namely he will favor American companies, the manufacturing industry, and particularly high-tech manufacturing.

Limiting Trade Reduces Efficiency and Competitiveness

First, it makes no sense to favor American companies over foreign companies. These are the types of policies that will drive plants for Toyota, BMW, Hyundai, Volkswagen, and Honda out of the American South.

Second, punishing companies for locating segments of the production chain in other countries makes those industries less efficient. This point requires a brief invocation of trade theory.

In 1817, David Ricardo noted that England could produce cloth quite efficiently, and Portugal was an adept producer of wine. Ricardo argued that each country could consume more of each if it specialized in its respective strong suit and traded. The case for free trade was born.

Ricardo's ideas still apply to a world of global supply chains, but our policy makers do not seem to understand. Consider an alternative history where England specializes in oranges instead of cloth, the Portuguese still all become vintners, and the two nations trade. Each nation ends up with more oranges and wine, which the tired workers promptly mix together and down as sangria.

Trade in parts, oranges and wine, allowed each country to consume more of the final product—sangria. While this example has not made it into the textbooks yet, it is extremely relevant in today's world. It means that punishing industries for taking part in global supply chains will make them less competitive.

Third, targeting industries for special treatment, like high-tech manufacturing, relies on outdated arguments for industrial policy. Some prominent economists from the 20th century, including Alfred Marshall and Paul Krugman, built a case for government protection or subsidy of key industries. Although intellectually defensible at the time, it has been largely undermined by the growth of supply chains.

The Global Economy Has Changed

The argument for industrial subsidies was based on the reality that some industries tend to cluster geographically. These clusters occur when industries share workers or inputs, or because knowledge spillovers occur between firms. Hollywood shares actors, Manhattan banks share securities lawyers, and tech geeks from different firms gather in Palo Alto [California] bars to discuss CPUs [central processing units], SEO [search engine optimization], JAR [Java Archive, a computer file format], and Python [a computer programming language] over beers. When an industry clusters for these reasons, economies of scale are created, and twice as many products can be produced for less than twice the money.

Moreover, these clusters can be quite arbitrary and dependent on historical whim. In 1541, John Calvin banned jewelry in Switzerland. As a result, Swiss jewelers started making watches, and they are still at it nearly 500 years later.

Could another country have been a more efficient watch capital? In the past, even if it could have, the industry would most likely not have moved. Since the economies of scale only work when the industry grows large, a bank would have had to finance the move of an entire industry to a new location and wait to reap future financial rewards. There's not a bank big enough.

Those who would advocate for an industrial policy of government intervention—through subsidies or import protection—presume that banks would be incapable of financing the relocation of an industry. However, studies of industrial policy throughout history have found few successes. The main reason for failure seems to be that policy makers just pick the wrong industries. They misapply the theory, pander to special interests, or lack the technical know-how to identify the industries that form clusters based on economies of scale. Krugman also has recognized these difficulties.

Globalized supply chains make the hard task of picking industries to support near impossible. Industrial clusters are becoming less prominent and less valuable. As business coordination costs fall due to improved communication technologies, the sub industries, like the manufacture of parts and components, are separating geographically from the headquarters, R&D, and distribution. A hollowed-out industry is not worth as large of a subsidy, and the proper industries to target will be harder to identify.

What's more, as industries break down into their sub-industries, it is more likely that a new firm will play a larger role in a sub-industry. Specialized workers and inputs will cluster around that firm, and knowledge spillovers will begin to occur across departments. While no bank is big enough to move an entire industry to a more efficient location, it might be able to move a sub-industry. Where capital markets work, governments should not meddle.

It Is Time for New Policies

No one can predict the future. The next communication or transportation revolutions will likely change the world as much as the Internet revolution has, and policy makers should not waste money predicting which industries will be valuable and which will still cluster.

The policies that President Obama outlined in his State of the Union address undermine the strength of America's economy and are the wrong way to react to the changing nature of trade. Action is necessary, but it should focus on preparing future generations to compete in a global marketplace through education reform and retraining current workers who lose their jobs due to trade. The best policy advice is always to put the Band-Aid where the cut is.

Periodical and Internet Sources Bibliography

The following articles have been selected to supplement the diverse views presented in this chapter.

Donald J. Boudreaux	"What Free Trade Really Does," *Pittsburgh Tribune-Review*, October 20, 2011.
Eric Martin and William McQuillen	"Congress Approves Biggest U.S. Trade Agreement Since 1994," Bloomberg, October 13, 2011. www.bloomberg.com.
John Nichols	"Obama Is Wrong, Wrong, Wrong About Free Trade," *Nation*, October 12, 2011.
William Poole	"Free Trade: Why Are Economists and Noneconomists So Far Apart?," *Federal Reserve Bank of St. Louis Review*, September/October 2004.
Uwe E. Reinhardt	"The Debate on Free Trade Continues," *Economix*, March 4, 2011. http://economix.blogs.nytimes.com.
Uwe E. Reinhardt	"How Convincing Is the Case for Free Trade?," *Economix*, February 18, 2011. http://economix.blogs.nytimes.com.
Jeffrey Snider	"The Financial Age of Free Trade," RealClearMarkets, April 13, 2012. www.realclearmarkets.com.
John Stossel	"Everyone Prospers with Free Trade," *Reason*, April 29, 2010.
David Zeiler	"Corporations Are the Real Winners When It Comes to Free Trade Agreements," MoneyMorning, October 14, 2011. http://moneymorning.com.

OPPOSING
VIEWPOINTS®
SERIES

CHAPTER 2

How Does Free Trade Impact Developing Countries?

| *"By spurring faster growth and rising incomes, trade and globalization also promote a rising consumer class and social progress."*

Free Trade Promotes Socially Progressive Values and Reduces Poverty in Developing Countries

Daniel T. Griswold

Daniel T. Griswold is associate director of the Cato Institute's Center for Trade Policy Studies. In the following viewpoint, taken from a chapter in his book Mad About Trade: Why Main Street America Should Embrace Globalization, *Griswold explains that the expansion of trade has created a global middle class, providing people worldwide with the means to pursue happier, healthier, and more productive lives. Griswold cites the rapid reduction in poverty found in developing nations and illustrates how this not only benefits those who are raised from poverty but also benefits Americans and others in the developed world who have a broader customer base and job opportunities around the world. In addition to the economic benefits, Griswold asserts, this growth has resulted in the spread of democratic and socially progressive values around the world as well as an increased desire for peace.*

As you read, consider the following questions:

1. What does Griswold cite as "middle-class, 'bourgeois' virtues"?

2. What does the viewpoint state that annual pharmaceutical sales will be by 2017?

3. What has helped to keep the peace in Europe for more than sixty years, according to Griswold?

A quiet revolution has changed the world for the better in the past three decades. The world is becoming more like us—more middle class, not just in what people wear and eat but in the way they live and think. Across a broad swath of what used to be called the Third World, incomes have been rising and poverty has been falling. Ownership of such middle-class tokens as a car, a refrigerator, and a computer are becoming more widespread. More kids are going to school, even college, leaving the farm for a better life in the city.

The impact of the emerging global middle class goes beyond daily living standards to shape the world in a way that is more hospitable for Americans today and for generations to come. An educated, property-owning middle class has become the backbone of democracy in a majority of the world's nations. Expanding commercial ties, coupled with representative government, have encouraged nations to live at peace with one another. The rising middle class has helped to spread middle-class, "bourgeois" virtues of thrift, industry, trustworthiness, and tolerance. . . .

A Rising Middle Class and Falling Poverty

The global economic downturn that reared its head in 2008 should not obscure the unprecedented material progress that globalization has brought to the world in recent years. Beginning in the 1990s, growth began to accelerate in China, India, and other emerging markets. The growth has been broadly based, creating the greatest expansion of the global middle class in human history. For the first time ever, a majority of the world's people now live in cities, and more people work in the service economy than in agriculture—milestones that the United States passed decades ago.

In sheer numbers, the World Bank calculates that 400 million people in less developed countries have already achieved an annual middle-class income of $16,800 to $72,000 per household. That number is on track to triple to 1.2 billion by 2030. By 2030, per capita income in the developing world will reach $11,000 a year in real terms—approximately the living standard in today's Czech Republic in the European Union. In a separate study released in July 2008, Goldman Sachs researchers Dominic Wilson and Raluca Dragusanu defined the middle class somewhat differently but came to the same conclusion: "An astonishing 2 billion people could join the global middle class by 2030!" They estimate the global middle class to be growing by about 70 million people a year, which is close to the annual growth in the world's population of 80 million. In other words, just about all of the world's net population growth is now occurring in the middle class.

The rise in the global middle class has gone hand in hand with a heartening drop in global poverty. The share of the world's population living in absolute poverty has been cut in half in the past 25 years. According to the World Bank, 52 percent of the world's population lived on the equivalent of $1.25 a day or less in 1981. By 2005, that share had dropped to 25 percent. For the first time in centuries, the total number of poor people living in the world has actually begun to decline in absolute numbers in the past two decades. The current global downturn has put that progress on pause temporarily, but we can expect it to resume when global growth returns to its more recent trend. . . .

In the early 1800s, an estimated 80 percent of the world's population lived on today's equivalent of $1.50 a day or less. It took more than 150 years of spreading globalization, industrialization, and technology to cut that share in half. The miracle is that mankind has managed to cut the ranks of the poor in half again, this time in a mere 25 years. Simply put, globalization and free trade have done more to lift people out of poverty than all the government foreign aid programs that ever existed.

If that were the sum of the story, it would be good news enough. But all sorts of positive things start to happen when the average per capita income in a developing country surpasses about $5,000 a year. Freed from the specter of starvation, people turn their attention to the relative luxuries of sending their children to school; accessing electrical, water, and sewer utilities for their homes; acquiring a TV, cell phone, household appliances, and a car; buying more health care and travel; and demanding protection for their property, a cleaner environment, and a larger voice in their own government. By spurring faster growth and rising incomes, trade and globalization also promote a rising consumer class and social progress.

For any American who has traveled recently to emerging economies, those are not hollow numbers. In places as diverse as Seoul, South Korea; Beijing, China; Mumbai, India; and Monterrey, Mexico, I have seen with my own eyes how ubiquitous automobiles, cell phones, laptop computers, and other consumer goods have become. More than a billion people in the world continue to live in deep poverty, but the real story of our time is how many of them are escaping to a life that more closely resembles our own.

If we look beneath the headlines, we can find stories of the emerging middle class. In Brazil, the shantytowns around its major cities, known as *favelas*, are being transformed into something resembling middle-class suburbs. In the metropolis of São Paulo, new apartment buildings are going up, and electricity, piped water, and sewer systems are being rapidly extended. A 2005 study of households in four *favelas* in São Paulo found that virtually all owned refrigerators and color TVs (often more than one), nearly half owned cell phones, and almost a third owned DVD players and cars. In the words of the *Economist* magazine, "They are members of a new middle class that is emerging almost overnight across Brazil and much of Latin America. Tens of millions of such people are the main beneficiaries of the region's hard-won economic stability and recent economic growth. Having left poverty behind, their incipient prosperity is driving the rapid growth of a mass consumer market in the region long notorious for the searing contrast between a small privileged elite and a poor majority."

More Customers and Business Partners

For Americans, the rise in the global middle class and the decline in global poverty have yielded direct and indirect benefits that will benefit our country and our children and grandchildren for decades to come. In the most direct way, a wealthier world means more potential customers and business partners for American producers and more suppliers competing to satisfy American consumers.

American companies are well positioned to sell their goods and services to a growing global market. American companies will increasingly find their best growth opportunities not in our mature domestic market but in rapidly expanding emerging economies. As hundreds of millions of people abroad join the global middle class, their appetite for and ability to buy the more sophisticated type of products and services offered by American producers will only grow. As the global middle class expands, the World Bank predicts that it "will participate actively in the global marketplace, demand world-class products, and aspire to international standards of higher education. That is, they would have the purchasing power to buy automobiles (perhaps second hand), purchase many consumer durables, and travel abroad."

Increased travel will bring more Chinese, Indians, and Latin Americans to the United States to spend dollars at our restaurants, hotels, and tourist attractions. Demand for airliners, including the new Boeing 787 Dreamliner, will predictably increase. Demand for U.S.-based medical and educational services will climb. By 2017, pharmaceutical sales in the biggest emerging markets are predicted to reach $300 billion a year, equal to today's sales in the top five European markets and the United States combined. America's leading drug companies are well positioned to meet the growing demand for an expanding array of medications and designer drugs. The Goldman Sachs study predicts rising global demand for meat, personal computers, financial services, insurance, and health care—sectors where American producers and brand names predominate.

The rising global middle class offers the best hope for America's automobile manufacturers. . . . Ford and General Motors are already selling more cars abroad than in the United States, and that trend will only grow. The Goldman Sachs team that has studied the emerging middle class notes that families in developing countries begin to buy automobiles when per capita income reaches $5,000, with the growth in demand peaking at $10,000 per capita. The number of cars on the road in the world is expected to climb from 600 million today to 2.9 billion by 2050. By 2030, there will be as many cars in China as there will be in the United States. If one out of ten cars is replaced each year, annual global car sales will also jump from just under 60 million in 2008 to nearly 300 million by 2050—a fivefold increase.

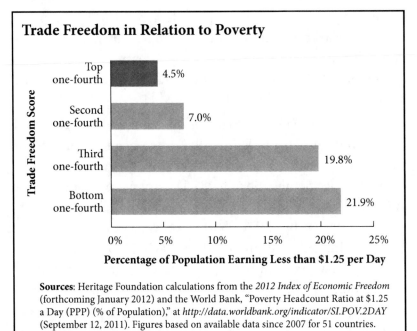

Trade Freedom in Relation to Poverty

Trade Freedom Score

- Top one-fourth — 4.5%
- Second one-fourth — 7.0%
- Third one-fourth — 19.8%
- Bottom one-fourth — 21.9%

Percentage of Population Earning Less than $1.25 per Day

Sources: Heritage Foundation calculations from the *2012 Index of Economic Freedom* (forthcoming January 2012) and the World Bank, "Poverty Headcount Ratio at $1.25 a Day (PPP) (% of Population)," at *http://data.worldbank.org/indicator/SI.POV.2DAY* (September 12, 2011). Figures based on available data since 2007 for 51 countries. PPP refers to purchasing power parity.

TAKEN FROM: Brittany Cobb, "Freer Trade, Greater Prosperity," *The Foundry*, October 14, 2011. http://blog.heritage.org.

In a more globalized world, our children will find more opportunities to work profitably with people around the world. . . .

Free Trade Nurtures a Free Society

Expanding trade and globalization deserve a share of the credit. Economic freedom and development have spread the tools of communication. Hundreds of millions of people in developing countries now have access to cell phones, the Internet, and satellite TV. Increased foreign travel and foreign investment have exposed them to a world of new friendships, ideas, and lifestyles. A more open and less controlled economy fosters the growth of "civil society"—including new businesses, independent labor unions, professional associations, and clubs, or what the great 18th-century British statesman

Edmund Burke called society's "little platoons." People in a free and open market tend to see people outside their ethnic and religious group not as threats but as potential customers and business partners. People learn to practice tolerance and compromise in their everyday lives, essential public traits for a democracy. Growth has also created a rising global middle class that is economically independent and politically aware. Freed from the daily shackles of toiling for subsistence, these middle-class families have turned their attention to such causes as securing property rights, improving the environment, and getting their kids through college. As people embrace the daily freedom of the marketplace and property ownership, they come to expect more freedom in the political sphere.

Nations open to the global economy are significantly more likely to enjoy greater political and civil freedoms than those countries that are relatively closed. Governments that grant their citizens a large measure of freedom to engage in international commerce find it increasingly difficult to deprive them of political and civil liberties, whereas governments that "protect" their citizens behind tariff walls and other barriers to international commerce find it much easier to deny those same liberties. A special panel commissioned by the WTO [World Trade Organization] to survey the state of the world trading system on the WTO's 10th anniversary rightly observed, "Generally, the marks of closed economies are lack of democracy and a free media, political repression, and the absence of opportunity for individuals to improve their lives through education, innovation, honest hard work and commitment.". . .

The spread of economic freedom, trade, globalization, and middle-class incomes has helped to lay the foundation for the flowering of democracy in such formerly authoritarian countries as South Korea, Taiwan, and Chile. It is not a coincidence that within a decade after the passage of NAFTA [North American Free Trade Agreement], one-party rule in Mexico was broken with the election of Vicente Fox in 2000. NAFTA helped to break the grip of the long-ruling PRI [Partido Revolucionario Institucional, or Institutional Revolutionary Party] over the economic life of the country. Now Mexico has become a vigorous multiparty democracy. In contrast, countries where political freedom and civil freedoms are in retreat, such as Venezuela and Zimbabwe, are also countries where governments are busy curtailing economic freedom. . . .

Free Trade's "Peace Dividend"

Our more globalized world has also yielded a "peace dividend." It may not be obvious when our daily news cycles are dominated by horrific images from the Gaza Strip, Afghanistan, and Darfur, but our more globalized world has somehow become a more peaceful world. The number of civil and international wars has dropped sharply in the past 15 years along with battle deaths. The reasons behind the retreat of war are complex, but again the spread of trade and globalization have played a key role. . . .

Free trade and globalization have promoted peace in three main ways. First, trade and globalization have reinforced the trend towards democracy, and democracies tend not to pick fights with each other. A second and even more potent way that trade has promoted peace is by raising the cost of war. As national economies become more intertwined, those nations have more to lose should war break out. War in a globalized world means not only the loss of human lives and tax dollars but also ruptured trade and investment ties that impose lasting damage on the economy. Trade and economic integration have helped to keep the peace in Europe for more than 60 years. More recently, deepening economic ties between China and Taiwan are drawing those two governments closer together and helping to keep the peace. Leaders on both sides of the Taiwan Strait seem to understand that reckless nationalism would jeopardize the dramatic economic progress that the region has enjoyed.

A third reason why free trade promotes peace is because it has reduced the spoils of war. Trade allows nations to acquire wealth through production and exchange rather than conquest of territory and resources. As economies develop, wealth is increasingly measured in terms of intellectual property, financial assets, and human capital. Such assets cannot be easily seized by armies. In contrast, hard assets such as minerals and farmland are becoming relatively less important in high-tech, service economies. If people need resources outside their national borders, say oil or timber or farm products, they can acquire them peacefully by freely trading what they can produce best at home. . . .

The Moral Case for Trade

As if it were not enough to argue that free trade has lifted millions out of poverty, strengthened human rights and democracy, and spread peace, let me make one more bold claim: Free trade and globalization encourage individuals to behave in better ways. The same "invisible hand" that turns our personal drive for betterment to the public's benefit also shapes our characters. The commercial and personal interactions with people from other countries that have come with globalization teach us tolerance, sympathy, humility, prudence, trustworthiness, and a spirit of service to our fellow human beings.

Success in the global marketplace requires winning the trust of strangers, proving reliability, and cooperating with people of differing language, culture, ethnicity, and race. The late Pope John Paul II, in a 1991 encyclical called *Centesimus Annus*, described the global economy as a sphere of activity where "people work with each other, sharing in a 'community of work' which embraces ever widening circles." In this expanding economic community, the pope observed, a market system encourages the virtues of "diligence, industriousness, prudence in undertaking reasonable risks, reliability and fidelity in interpersonal relationships, as well as courage in carrying out decisions which are difficult and painful but necessary, both for the overall working of a business and in meeting possible setbacks." As markets expand across borders and into new regions of the world, those "bourgeois virtues" increase at the expense of such vices as sloth, mistrust, duplicity, prejudice, and xenophobic nationalism.

The expansion of global markets reinforces fair play and the rule of law. Citizens and officials are not exposed to the temptation to game the system and seek special favors. When imports are controlled by arbitrary tariffs, quotas, and licensing regimes, opportunities multiply for graft and bribery. In less developed countries, it is not uncommon that citizens who want a consumer good or need a spare part must seek the favor of someone in authority. Barriers to trade can also promote smuggling, underground supply chains, and criminal cartels. For all those reasons, studies show that nations that are more open economically tend to be less corrupt.

Historically, those cities and countries at the forefront of international trade were also among the most open and tolerant societies of their day. Venice in the 1400s and the Dutch Republic in the 1600s were the leading commercial centers of their eras. They each provided freedom and legal protection to Jews and religious dissenters. Their citizens learned to welcome people of differing religions and races because intolerance was, among its other shortcomings, bad for business. Today, as we have seen, societies open to trade are more likely to be open to freedom of religion and speech and political pluralism.

In the end, the argument in favor of free trade comes down to one of basic justice. If an American wants to trade what he has produced for something a person or group of people in another country have produced, our government should not interfere. To use the power of government to forbid a transaction that is beneficial to the two parties involved is to violate the sovereignty of free individuals. Trade barriers rob people of the rightful fruits of their own labor, distributing the spoils to other people with no moral claim to the confiscated wealth other than political power.

Free trade gives to each person sovereign control over that which is his own. In his 1849 essay, "Protectionism and Communism," the French political economist Frédéric Bastiat wrote,

> Every citizen who has produced or acquired a product should have the option of applying it immediately to his own use or of transferring it to whoever on the face of the earth agrees to give him in exchange the object of his desires. To deprive him of this option when he has committed no act contrary to public order and good morals, and solely to satisfy the convenience of another citizen, is to legitimize an act of plunder and to violate the law of justice.

That should be reason enough for Americans to demand that the last fetters on our freedom to trade be removed.

*"By undermining the Mexican economy,
[the North American Free Trade Agree-
ment] has greatly strengthened the drug
cartels, which thrive on social instability."*

Free Trade Policies Create a Culture of Crime and Devastate Impoverished Countries

David T. Rowlands

David T. Rowlands is a frequent contributor to Green Left
Weekly *and works as an educator in Australia. In the following
viewpoint, Rowlands argues that the North American Free Trade
Agreement (NAFTA) has created economic hardship for Mexi-
cans and has left many of them with no option but to turn to
criminal enterprises to survive. This, Rowlands declares, is the
direct result of corporations that sought to profit from cheap labor and rock-bottom prices on land and natural resources, and is
the direct cause of the war between rival drug gangs and law enforcement agencies that has resulted in the deaths of so many
Mexican people. The connection between NAFTA, the Mexican*

drug war, and rising poverty is neither acknowledged nor addressed by either the US or Mexican governments, Rowlands claims.

As you read, consider the following questions:

1. What does Rowlands say completed the liquidation of Mexico's traditional rural base?

2. What does Bruce Livesey note is the second biggest export and industry in Mexico?

3. According to Rowlands, what does the decision to use a discredited military solution to the problem of narco-trafficking indicate about Washington's real intention?

In Mexico, a war involving rival drug gangs, law enforcement agencies and the national army has officially claimed 23,000 lives since 2006.

This figure does not include the many thousands of innocent people who have been "disappeared" by police and army units.

The violence can be directly attributed to the corrosive impact of the North American Free Trade Agreement (NAFTA).

NAFTA was signed on January 1, 1994, between the United States, Canada, and Mexico with the aim of removing trade and investment barriers between these nations.

NAFTA was sold to the Mexican people as "a ticket out of Third World poverty", but its underlying aim was conquest by stealth.

Over the past 16 years, NAFTA has helped worsen grotesque wealth disparities, rampant corruption and environmental destruction across Mexico. It has helped create millions of internal economic refugees.

A Loss of Farms Drives Farmers to Crime

Within a year of NAFTA's implementation, millions of small farmers in Mexico lost their livelihoods due to the rise in agricultural imports from north of the border.

Unable to compete with the dumping of heavily subsidised US agribusiness grain, Mexico's rural economy collapsed and rural poverty rates soared above 80%.

This disaster was no accident, but part of the game plan to turn the general population into a cheap source of labour for North American corporations.

To complete the liquidation of Mexico's traditional rural base, crucial land rights provisions in the constitution were overturned at the insistence of US negotiators.

The loss of traditional communal estates (*ejidos*) allowed huge swathes of territory to be taken over by profit-hungry multinational corporations seeking access to timber, oil, minerals and hydroelectricity.

Driven off their lands by mislabelled "free market forces", displaced farmers fled to the northern border zone.

There, they joined hundreds of thousands of Mexico's urban unemployed, themselves the victims of "restructuring" and the International Monetary Fund–dictated privatisation of state assets that accompanied NAFTA.

The expanded network of frontier sweat-shop factories (*maquiladoras*) serviced the needs of the US market. Low wages, no unions and intensive exploitation fuelled the so-called Mexican boom of the 1990s.

However, many of these jobs evaporated when China entered the World Trade Organization, offering corporations even cheaper labour costs than Mexico.

In recent years, the Mexican unemployment rate has risen even higher under the impact of the global financial crisis and the US recession.

NAFTA Has Devastated Mexico

NAFTA has had bad consequences for workers in all three participating countries, but it is in Mexico that NAFTA has caused the most devastation.

Meaningful investment in public services has become almost nonexistent. The economy is locked into a pattern of subsistence wages for the majority and obscene profits for the corporate ruling elite and foreign interests.

Workers' share of the gross domestic product is lower than at any time in modern Mexican history—a statistic that reveals the true nature of the NAFTA project.

By undermining the Mexican economy, NAFTA has greatly strengthened the drug cartels, which thrive on social instability.

Bruce Livesey, a US investigative journalist who has written extensively about Mexico's crisis, told Real News on September 1 [2010] that the "displaced population in northern Mexico . . . couldn't go back to the land to make a living".

He said, "Increasingly their only economic opportunity was the drug trade. . . . Now you have a significant portion of the Mexican population that is involved."

Livesey noted: "The second biggest export and industry in Mexico is the drug trade, after oil production."

Supplied with a limitless pool of desperate, unemployed recruits, the cartels have taken advantage of increased truck flows through the US border to make Mexico the main smuggling conduit for Andean cocaine. The trade is worth at least US$50 billion a year.

This Is a "War for Drugs"

With huge profits at stake, competing factions such as the Sinaloa and Zeta cartels have engaged in an all-out war for control of the drug corridors around the border city of Juárez since the early 2000s.

The North American Free Trade Agreement and Its Impact on the Mexican Economy

When the North American Free Trade Agreement (NAFTA) effectively started on January 1, 1994, it pushed Mexico into global economic status, effectively as part of the U.S. production chain. . . .

Following NAFTA's inception, more than 85 percent of exports and the majority of imports were partnered with the U.S. market. Mexican exports have grown tremendously, up to $292 billion in 2008, five times what it has been in years past. This however does not translate over to money for the average Mexican; instead, the growth feeds the multinational corporations who have moved into Mexico, pursuing cheaper labor prices. Most of the small business owners around the country have been driven out by larger companies. Low-wage jobs and unpromising careers in entrepreneurship have caused many Mexican citizens to move north into the U.S., looking for better opportunities.

Wade Rice, "Mexican Drug War: Free Trade in a Country Plagued by Our Own Consumption," Neumann Business Review, 2010, pp. 32–33.

On orders from Washington, the government of Mexican president Felipe Calderón has sent in soldiers in the name of fighting the "war on drugs". The reality is very different.

There have been allegations made that the national army favours the well-established Sinaloa group, whose corrupt links extend all the way to the top.

Investigative journalist Diego Enrique Osorno told Al Jazeera on February 21 [2010]: "There are no important detentions of Sinaloa cartel members. But the government is hunting down adversary groups, new players in the world of drug trafficking."

Charles Bowden, the US author of this year's *Murder City: Ciudad Juarez and the Global Economy's New Killing Fields*, told *Democracy Now!* on April 14 that it was not a war on drugs, but a "war for drugs".

He said this war was being funded by the US government to the tune of $500 million a year.

As in Colombia, the so-called drug war not only lines the pockets of a corrupt regime, it also provides a useful pretext to clamp down on any form of dissent. Bowden said: "What we've done is what we've done historically: We've gotten on the wrong side."

"We're not siding with the Mexican people. We're siding with the people that own the country and terrorise them."

The US and Mexican Governments Are Concealing the Truth

The Mexican government and its Washington masters have failed to acknowledge the direct connection between NAFTA policies and Mexico's slide into chaos.

Opting instead for a discredited military solution to the problem of narco-trafficking, Washington's real intention is to consolidate its grip on the Mexican state.

In an April 26 GlobalResearch.ca article, Mike Whitney said: "The drug war is the mask behind which the real policy is concealed. The United States is using all the implements in its national security toolbox to integrate Mexico into a North America Uberstate. . . .

"That means the killing in Juárez will continue until Washington's objectives are achieved."

It's not a war on drugs, but a war on the poor.

Last year was the worst year for drug violence in Mexico on record. There were more than 9,600 recorded victims, most of them innocent bystanders.

This year looks set to surpass this grim tally—and more drugs than ever before are pouring across the Mexican border. This includes hundreds of millions of dollars worth of Sinaloa-supplied cocaine intended for the Australian market.

"*In trying to capture the benefits of free trade while avoiding the costs, it is important to link free trade agreements both to provisions to reduce poverty and to provisions to mitigate environmental problems.*"

Balanced Free Trade Can Reduce World Poverty and Threats from Climate Change

Nicole J. Hassoun

Nicole J. Hassoun is an assistant professor of philosophy and a member of the Center for Ethics and Policy at Carnegie Mellon University. In the following viewpoint, Hassoun asserts that free trade has the potential to lower both poverty and environmental threats. She explains the various links between poverty and environmental concerns, such as global warming, and illustrates that those who are interested in expanding trade should be concerned about both issues. Hassoun outlines the main arguments for and against using trade as a means of addressing poverty and climate change, and she concludes that no argument can persuasively make the case that free trade would have either completely positive or completely negative effects on these issues. Nevertheless,

Nicole J. Hassoun, "Free Trade, Poverty, and the Environment," *Public Affairs Quarterly*, vol. 22, no. 4, October 2008, pp. 353, 355–356, 360–364, 369. http://www.hss.cmu.edu.

she maintains, if trade policies are carefully drafted with the goal of mitigating both poverty and environmental threats, then free trade can be exceptionally helpful in battling these two devastating global issues. Further, Hassoun argues that the benefits of trade for the poor and for the environment can be supported by private companies and individual consumers as well as by government policy makers.

As you read, consider the following questions:

1. By what year, according to the viewpoint, are developing countries expected to emit more carbon dioxide than industrialized countries?

2. What did the World Bank estimate that fossil fuel consumption subsidies totaled in 1992, according to the viewpoint?

3. How could supporting and expanding fair trade–certified goods benefit the poor and the environment, according to Hassoun?

Proponents of free trade argue that the moral case for free trade is strong in light of the fact that it is the quickest way to reduce poverty. In fact, the view that free trade is good for the poor is so widely accepted that it is hard to get a word in edgewise. The *Economist*, the World Bank, and the International Monetary Fund accept this claim with nearly dogmatic ideological passion. Many philosophers, economists, and lawyers are similarly convinced that the case for free trade is strong because it will reduce poverty. For instance, Fernando Teson and Jonathan Klick follow many economists in suggesting that the argument from comparative advantage [referring to an economic theory that states that all countries can prosper from trading freely because some countries are able to produce goods and provide services more efficiently than others] largely vindicates this conclusion. On the other hand, opponents of free trade counter, just as dogmatically, that free trade will lead to environmental problems like climate change. For instance, some advance the race-to-the-bottom argument on which free trade will put downward pressure on regulatory standards increasing pollution and, so, environmental problems. . . .

Poverty and the Environment

A concern for the poor and the environment are connected. Those who care about poverty have reason to care about the environment. Natural disasters or famines have harmed billions of poor people in the last decade; hundreds of thousands died as a result. Hundreds of thousands of poor people also die every year from infectious diseases like malaria. Environmental problems like climate change are likely to contribute to the devastation such diseases, disasters, and famines bring. Epidemiologists predict increasing malaria rates, climatologists argue that there will be a rising number of droughts and floods, and geologists suggest that there will be more natural disasters. The poorest are likely to suffer most from these changes. They are the most exposed and the least able to adapt to changing environmental conditions. Those who care about poverty have reason to care about the environment.

Conversely, those who care about the environment have reason to care about poverty. The poor, collectively, contribute a lot to environmental problems like climate change by using scarce sinks (like forests) and other nonrenewable resources. Swidden, or slash and burn, agriculture—usually employed by poor farmers who want to plant crops or raise cattle on marginal lands—causes immense deforestation. Poor people, who do not have access to electricity or gas, burn a lot of wood and coal to cook their meals and heat their homes. Moreover, as developing countries start using more fossil fuel, their emissions will rise. Developing countries are expected to emit more carbon dioxide than industrialized countries by about

2018. Those who care about environmental problems like climate change have reason to care about poverty.

Because poverty and environmental quality are connected in these ways, if free trade benefits the poor, it will probably mitigate environmental problems like climate change, at least a little. Similarly, if free trade harms the environment it will probably increase poverty some. Of course, even if free trade increases environmental problems and this harms the poor in some ways, free trade may benefit the poor in other ways. Free trade's net impact on the poor may even be positive. Similarly, even if free trade decreases poverty and this benefits the environment in some ways, free trade may harm the environment in other ways. Free trade's net impact on the environment may even be negative. Still, conflict is by no means certain. Free trade may generally be good for both the poor and the environment or bad for both. When we consider arguments for and against free trade we, thus, need to consider the interaction between free trade's impact on the poor and its impact on the environment. . . .

It Makes Sense to Support Trade Policies That Help the Environment and the Poor

We can use neither the argument from comparative advantage nor the race-to-the-bottom argument to decide what free trade's impact on the poor or the environment will be. . . . In practice, free trade probably has mixed effects. Some free trade reforms probably benefit the poor and the environment while others hurt the poor and the environment. Some free trade reforms probably benefit the poor and hurt the environment while others benefit the environment and hurt the poor. All other things being equal, the obligation to reduce world poverty and mitigate environmental problems provides reason to support reforms only insofar as they help the poor and the environment. . . .

We might consider free trade in the energy sector to see how free trade is likely to have mixed impacts on the environment. Energy use is the main contributor to climate change. Burning coal contributes about two-fifths of the world's carbon emissions. Many countries subsidize use of such traditional energy resources. The World Bank estimated that fossil fuel *consumption* subsidies alone amounted to more than $200 billion dollars in 1992. Such subsidies can reduce prices for traditional energy sources encouraging consumption and thus increasing pollution. So, reducing these subsidies may help reduce climate change and other environmental problems. Still, some energy subsidies may benefit the environment. It would probably be unfortunate if subsidies for some renewable and sustainable energy sources decline. Though, even here, the case is not so clear. It depends on which renewable energy source and what environmental problems we care about.

The details vary and are difficult to work out. We must keep in mind the fact that reforms that benefit the environment (or the poor) may harm the poor (or the environment). Subsidies of traditional energy resources, for instance, may be very important for the poor. This much should be clear, however: Some free trade reforms can reduce poverty. Some can mitigate environmental problems. Most reforms probably have mixed impacts. In light of obligations to reduce poverty and mitigate environmental problems there is (ceteris paribus [all things being equal]) reason to support those reforms that both reduce poverty and environmental problems. There are likely many such reforms. And, when a reform that has some good effects (on the poor or the environment) also has some bad effects (on the poor or the environment) there is reason to see if there is a way to capture the good effects while avoiding the bad ones.

There will almost certainly be some times when there is reason to support a policy that requires trade-offs between ameliorating poverty and mitigating environmental problems.

Sometimes there may even be reason to support such a policy over one that benefits both the poor and the environment. A policy that requires trade-offs may be much more cost effective than one that does not or may help us fulfill other moral obligations we may have. Sometimes, it may even be better to spend the available funds on reducing poverty a lot at a slight cost to the environment rather than making minor improvements that help both the poor and the environment. We need a theory about how to deal with policies that require trade-offs. Still, this should not stop us from trying to find constructive and creative alternatives to unfettered free trade that capture the benefits of free trade for both the poor and the environment while avoiding associated costs.

Restructuring the Rules of Trade

Believing that there is an obligation to reduce poverty and mitigate environmental problems does not give one a reason to support unfettered free trade or isolationism. Instead, there is reason to support those policies (protectionist or not) that reduce poverty and environmental problems. Whether or not a particular alternative should ultimately be implemented will depend on many things. It will depend, for instance, on what other options there are (among other things). The seemingly innocuous proposition that there is reason to consider embracing those policies (protectionist or not) that enable people to avoid poverty and help the environment directly contravenes current international law embodied in the WTO [World Trade Organization]. Although the WTO does make some provisions for the poor ..., these provisions are not as broad as those we are considering. So, we must consider how it is possible to restructure the rules of trade embodied in the WTO or work around them to better reduce poverty and mitigate environmental problems.... Holding everything else equal, if there are defensible ways to restructure the rules of trade so that they better help the poor and the environment, current WTO rules are unjustifiable.

In trying to capture the benefits of free trade while avoiding the costs, it is important to link free trade agreements both to provisions to reduce poverty and to provisions to mitigate environmental problems. Otherwise reforms that help the poor may harm the environment and vice versa. So, it might be good to change the rules of the WTO so that they *compensate* the poorest when they are hurt by free trade *and* create analogous means of mitigating environmental problems. . . .

The WTO might also create programs to compensate poor *individuals* who lose from free trade or require countries to implement such programs. Such compensation should take a long-term perspective on helping their beneficiaries avoid poverty by helping them adapt to changing economic conditions. . . .

When a trade reform is likely to hurt the environment, the WTO might require compensatory measures to reduce this impact. If, for instance, a free trade agreement is expected to increase trade in wood products, thus hastening climate change, the WTO might require countries to plant new trees.

Again, it is important that the WTO attend to its policies' impacts on the poor and the environment together. A reform that compensates the poor may still harm the environment. A reform that compensates for damage to the environment may still harm the poor.

There are also many other ways of restructuring the rules of global trade so that they *proactively* reduce *both* poverty *and* environmental problems. Christian Barry and Sanjay Reddy argue that there is reason to link free trade agreements to agreements to improve labor standards and wages in developing countries. If this scheme were extended, the rules of trade might also require linking free trade agreements to agreements to improve environmental regulations. Linkage could both help the poor and reduce environmental problems.

Similarly, the WTO might be altered so that it allows countries to use trade policy to unilaterally improve the position of the poor while also helping the environment. Consider a simple example of how imposing a trade barrier may both help the poor and the environment. Suppose that *Destitute* is a very large country and raises a tariff against marsupials from any other country. This will reduce demand for foreign marsupials in Destitute. Producers in Destitute who sell their goods domestically will benefit since they will be able to sell marsupials at higher prices. Consumers in Destitute will lose out because they will have to pay these higher prices. Any producers in Destitute selling overseas will make less since more marsupials will be sold overseas at lower cost. Still, the money captured from the foreign marsupials that are sold in Destitute, plus the extra revenue the producers make in Destitute, may leave Destitute as a whole better off. Suppose the following conditions hold as well: The poorest in Destitute do not buy marsupials but produce them for domestic sale and the poorest in foreign countries do not produce marsupials but consume them. Since different countries have different preferences for food and different technologies, this may be quite realistic. On these conditions, the impact of this tariff could be good for all poor people in present generations. Suppose, further, that marsupial production produces a lot of greenhouse gas. Since the tariff would decrease overall production of marsupials, it might even help poor people in future generations and benefit the environment. Although this is, of course, a hypothetical example, similar tariffs might bring great gains to the poor and the environment. Even rich countries might justifiably help the poor and the environment using trade policy unilaterally. If WTO rules allowed countries to use such trade barriers, trade policy could provide a useful tool for reducing poverty and environmental problems.

Nongovernmental Organizations and Individuals Can Help Support Positive Outcomes

Those with a libertarian bent might object that this presupposes the possibility of fine-tuned social engineering. It is not clear that we have the knowledge we need to decide whether allowing particular countries to implement particular tariffs will benefit the poor and the environment. Moreover, it would be expensive and difficult to analyze the prospects for different tariffs bringing such benefits. Perhaps constraints on the free market are unjustifiable for this reason. The WTO has enough to do without evaluating every possible tariff.

Although there is something to this objection, it is not clear that it is correct. It might not be very expensive or difficult to figure out that some trade barriers will benefit both the poor and the environment. Nor need the WTO be responsible for doing so. Perhaps the WTO could allow countries to declare any trade barriers intended to benefit the poor and the environment as long as they are prepared to justify their barriers if challenged. Nongovernmental organizations might, then, help developing countries that lack the capacity or resources to do the requisite econometric analysis find new ways to benefit the poor and the environment. Alternately, to minimize abuse, the WTO might just permit resource-rich developing countries to implement trade barriers to benefit the poor and the environment, subject to random review. Although the details would need to be worked out carefully, it is at least worth considering the possibility of allowing trade barriers that do benefit the poor and the environment.

Finally, even individuals can promote free trade that does not increase poverty or environmental problems. They might, for instance, buy fair trade–certified goods. Goods sold as fair trade certified must meet certain standards. At a minimum, they must be produced by people paid a living wage in an environmentally sustainable way. Purchasing fair trade–certified goods will probably not completely solve the problems free trade can cause for the poor or the environment, but it could do a lot of good if it leads to rising production standards. The collective impact of individual choices can be large. Altering some trade policy may help the fair trade movement. The WTO might require countries to label goods produced in sustainable ways that help the poor as fair trade certified. But, even unaided consumer action is powerful. Boycotts of tuna not caught in dolphin-safe nets changed the tuna-fishing industry when the WTO failed to do so. Purchasing fair trade–certified goods may help those whose lives our consumption choices most directly impact while also mitigating environmental problems. . . .

Hundreds of thousands of people protest against the WTO because they believe that the race-to-the-bottom argument shows free trade will decimate the environment, while equally passionate advocates of free trade cite the argument from comparative advantage as evidence that free trade will ameliorate world poverty. Neither argument alone can make or undercut the case for free trade. The potential benefits of free trade for ameliorating world poverty and environmental problems are large. But, there are also good reasons to be skeptical of the claim that free trade is always the best way to reduce poverty and mitigate environmental problems. Trade-related adjustment assistance programs, linkage, trade barriers, and consumer movements (like the fair trade movement) may be necessary and desirable. The WTO's proscription of many of these alternatives may be unjustifiable. At least, these alternatives merit consideration if they are the most efficient means of helping the poor and appropriate institutional safeguards are put in place to prevent abuse.

> "Although both [the United States and Colombia] have tried to tackle the issue of human rights violations, at the end of the day they are more concerned with their economic interests and hold those to be much more of a priority."

Free Trade Agreements Fail to Adequately Protect Workers' Rights or Reduce Crime

Robert Valencia

Robert Valencia is a research fellow with the Council on Hemispheric Affairs (COHA). In the following viewpoint, Valencia discusses why Democratic congressmen have expressed objections to the US free trade agreement with Colombia on the grounds that Colombia has failed to protect union leaders against attacks from insurgents or paramilitary groups. Such activities are not only allowed by Colombian governments, Valencia reports, but are also condoned by US companies that hire insurgents to protect their property. Because the United States needs cooperation from Colombia to fight the problem of illegal drug trading and

Colombia needs financial assistance from the United States to support its economic development, Valencia argues, the problems of human rights violations each country supports, either directly or indirectly, are overlooked, and policies are enforced to protect workers from rights abuses or victimization by brutal regimes. Furthermore, Valencia notes, several groups oppose a US-Colombian trade agreement on the grounds that it will not benefit the economy or workers in either country but would only serve as a tool for the United States to gain political leverage in Latin America.

As you read, consider the following questions:

1. According to the viewpoint, what agreement did the United States and Colombia sign in 2002, and what did it offer?

2. Why have Republicans opposed President Obama's extension of the Trade Adjustment Assistance program, according to the viewpoint?

3. According to the viewpoint, what is necessary from both sides to guarantee a fair and equal agreement of trade to workers and consumers in both the United States and Colombia?

In recent years, Colombia has signed a bundle of free trade agreements with Chile, Peru, Mexico, and Canada while seeking membership of the Asia-Pacific Economic Cooperation (APEC) and opening markets with Japan and South Korea. Bogotá [the capital of Colombia] now seeks new markets for its products because of the diplomatic and economic stalemate with Venezuela, Colombia's second trading partner. Nevertheless, Colombia has been actively seeking a trade agreement with the United States, and despite a seemingly clear path for its approval, it also entails some controversy.

It's worth noting that in 2002, Colombia and the United States signed the Andean Trade Promotion and Drug Eradication Act, which offers a way to foster human development and at the same time controls cocaine production. Both countries also signed the controversial Plan Colombia in 1998. For some Colombians, and particularly for the last several administrations in both countries, a free trade agreement with the United States would involve unconditional support from Colombians, given their long-standing common struggle against the drug trade.

Several congressmen, particularly Democrats, often have been reluctant to support this agreement. They have based their argument on the fact that Colombia does not adequately protect union leaders from the insurgents or paramilitaries. They are not the only ones dragging their feet on the trade accord. The Washington Office on Latin America (WOLA) presented what they called an "argument" three years ago where, aside from corroborating on the crimes committed against union leaders, it underscored that the peasants' displacement would also increase the expropriation of lands in, if need be, a more violent manner in order to "benefit agro-export crops such as palm oil, which would benefit from the trade agreement." The previously mentioned report adds that a possible agreement would most likely adversely affect the poor, weaken regional development, and even pose a national security risk.

The Cases of Coca-Cola and Dole

Notwithstanding, this statement, alongside those extended by a number of congressmen, seemed to overlook that several U.S. companies were permissive regarding insurgent activities by bribing them to protect their own property, such as the contested cases of Coca-Cola and Dole. One of the most notorious cases of neglect came from Chiquita Brands, the multinational successor of the United Fruit Company, which in a "bona fide" act went to the Department of Justice and acknowledged its own involvement with the paramilitaries. Despite paying a USD [US dollar] 25 million fine to the U.S. government that had scrutinized the company's activities, mounting pressure from victims of the paramilitaries along with Colombian state officials have led Chiquita Brands to give up its market share in Colombia's banana industry.

All in all, despite the fact that the Colombian and U.S government officials were aware of the human rights violations that had occurred within the operations of companies like Chiquita [Brands], Coca-Cola, and Dole, redress has been delayed. Why does the Colombian government not resort to fury against the U.S. even in the face of these notorious violations? Although both countries have tried to tackle the issue of human rights violations, at the end of the day they are more concerned with their economic interests and hold those to be much more of a priority. Colombia will not thrive without aid from the U.S. (third largest recipient of U.S. assistance), and the U.S. will never be able to tackle the root of the drug problem unless they cooperate with Colombia.

There are other international bodies that support the benefits and advantages that an agreement will bring to Colombia. According to an article published by Sergio Arboleda University in Bogotá, Colombia, the World Bank strongly believes that as a result of free trade, forty-four million Colombians "can enjoy a large quantity of goods and services at lower prices and better quality." Former president Álvaro Uribe [Vélez] assured that intellectual property of medicine would not be affected by the free trade agreement.

Colombia as a Foothold for Trade Agreements in Latin America

For some organizations like the Independent Institute, a trade agreement with Colombia would not make too much of a difference for the improvement of the U.S. economy. In reality, such treatment will bring several benefits stateside, not only because of the reduction on taxes on goods and services, but also because the United States will be able to rely upon Colombia as a way to exercise U.S. influence within Latin America, at a time when it is on the wane. Meanwhile, a number of left-leaning Latin American nations like Venezuela, Nicaragua, Ecuador and Bolivia are likely to continue to drift away from Uncle Sam. Furthermore, Brazil has become a driving force, not only of its own growth but for the rest of the region as well, thus ending up with an inevitable decrease of Washington's economic leverage in the region.

Colombians are not the only ones concerned about imminent trade approval with one nation or another. Widespread skepticism is prevalent over how the Colombian free trade agreement, along with the two other agreements that are also up for signature and have been on the congressional back burner (those of Panama and South Korea), would benefit the U.S. economy. Doubts arise from the fact that many U.S. corporations are outsourcing their workforce, increasing the nation's already battered employment prospects. Case in point: General Motors and Ford have moved part of their operations to Mexico, which in turn has generated a labor crisis in Detroit and its surrounding areas.

Consequently, in light of these mixed signals, the [Barack] Obama administration is contemplating a series of measures with its trade agreement bills, in order to help more of those who have lost their jobs as a result of outsourcing. But Republican legislators, staunch supporters of free trade, consistently have expressed their disdain for the extension of the Trade Adjustment Assistance [program], in opposing President Obama's aspirations to link stimulus packages to the treaties.

Modest Changes Can Achieve Fairness

Even in the midst of such uncertainty, how can both Washington and Bogotá guarantee a fair and equal treatment of trade to workers and consumers in both countries? It starts with something modest: As the bipartisan agreement in 2007 suggests, both the Colombian and U.S. governments should abide by the rules so as to benefit the workforce of both countries. Both the U.S. and Colombian governments have expressed concern regarding the lack of protection of union leaders in Colombia. Washington has admonished that Bogotá must protect the labor rights of its own union leaders, who have been cut down by the fusillades of right-wing vigilantes in the country. Bogotá must follow Obama's insistence that abuses of labor in either country will not be tolerated. It is imperative for Colombia to make greater strides to abolish human rights abuses while renovating its highways, ports, and overall physical infrastructure to better channel the movement of trade. In addition, Colombia must protect the country's *campesinos* [farm laborers] and their standard of living in the event that their farm products lose value and force an increase in the migration to already sprawling urban slums. Even if such formulae are able to challenge the existing debate surrounding the advantages of the pending free trade agreement and the degree to which the agreement reflects mutual benefits for both the United States and Colombia, we will still be at the beginning of fashioning an equitable trade policy.

Periodical and Internet Sources Bibliography

The following articles have been selected to supplement the diverse views presented in this chapter.

Jagdish Bhagwati	"Free Trade Ad Nauseum," *Project Syndicate*, February 29, 2012. www.project-syndicate.org.
Cat Contiguglia	"Is Fair Trade Good?," *Prague Post*, May 25, 2011.
Greg Grandin	"White House to Push for Colombia Free Trade Treaty: Expect Body Count to Rise," *Nation*, February 3, 2011.
Chico Harlan	"In Japan, Possible Free Trade Deal Comes with an Argument," *Washington Post*, October 30, 2011.
Quynh Hoa	"EU Free Trade Agreement to Boost VN Economy," *Viet Nam News*, March 3, 2012.
Charles Johnson	"I'm Against Free Trade Agreements Because I'm for Free Trade," *Bleeding Heart Libertarians*, August 22, 2011. http://bleedingheart libertarians.com.
Wanki Moon	"Is Agriculture Compatible with Free Trade?," *Ecological Economics*, vol. 71, November 15, 2011.
William Neuman	"A Question of Fairness," *New York Times*, November 23, 2011.
Anup Shah	"Free Trade and Globalization," Global Issues, November 7, 2011. www.globalissues.org.
Abdi Tsegaye	"Ethiopia: Nation Not Ready to Join Free Trade Area After Decade," *Addis Fortune* (Ethiopia), February 26, 2012.

OPPOSING
VIEWPOINTS®
SERIES

CHAPTER 3

What Is the Effect of Free Trade on Human Rights and Labor Regulations?

Chapter Preface

U S trade policy is almost always debated in terms of economic utility, but there are those who hold that many overbearing regulations can give too much power to a few potentially corrupt ruling regimes, lock out those smaller producers who would benefit from a broader trade spectrum, and prevent innovative ideas from flourishing. On the other hand, some argue that too much deregulation can lead to corporations being able to undermine basic social and human rights; can allow misuse of human industry; and can lead to environmental damage, often without accountability.

Trade is an absolute necessity if a nation's economy and people are to thrive. The question is, is this trade supposed to be free, or should trade be governed by protectionism?

Daniel T. Griswold believes that behind the statistics and anecdotes of the advantages and disadvantages of free trade versus protectionism are moral assumptions about human nature, the sovereignty of the individual, and the role of government in a free society. All discussions must center on the impact of trade upon humankind.

In his article "Seven Moral Arguments for Free Trade," Griswold gives readers seven arguments that he believes form a moral case for favoring free trade. These seven arguments are:

1. Free trade respects the dignity and sovereignty of the individual.

2. Free trade restrains the power of the state.

3. Free trade encourages individuals to cultivate moral values.

4. Free trade brings people together across distance and cultures.

5. Free trade encourages other basic human rights, such as freedom of speech and religion.

6. Free trade fosters peace by raising the cost of war.

7. Free trade feeds and clothes the poor.

"When all these arguments are weighed," Griswold concludes, "it should become clear that a policy of free trade is moral as well as efficient. Free trade limits the power of the state and enhances the freedom, autonomy, and self-responsibility of the individual. It promotes virtuous and responsible personal behavior. It brings people together in 'communities of work' that cross borders and cultures. It opens the door for ideas and evangelism. It undermines the authority of dictators by expanding the freedom, opportunity, and independence of the people they try to control. It promotes peace among nations. It helps the poor to feed and care for themselves and creates a better future for their children. For which of these virtues should we reject free trade?"

Other commentators oppose Griswold's assessment and advance a moral case *against* free trade. Michael J. Hurd writes in *Capitalism Magazine*: "If you engage in trade with the unfree country, then you enable its government to pretend that dictatorship can work. You assist in the aid of nonfreedom. . . . With regard to China, trading with dictatorships means: You assist the unfree government in building up its military muscle, thereby threatening peaceful, free countries such as the one in which you live." Hurd also refutes those who argue that free trade is morally defensible and will ultimately lead to freer societies in the countries participating in free global trade: "Some argue that helping victims of a dictatorship build an underground economy will help those victims eventually emerge free. But where's the evidence for this claim? China remains as unfree as ever after years of economic liberalization and favorable trade status with the U.S. . . . If anything, China seems to be getting more dictatorial in recent years. [Fidel] Castro has kept Cuba under dictatorship for four decades now, despite the presence of an underground economy to keep the country from completely going under."

Blogger Nat-Wu agrees with Hurd and dismisses arguments that free trade creates opportunities and higher living standards for workers. Nat-Wu observes: "If you take two closed economies and open them up so that they can trade components, obviously the business owner who pays his workers more will seek to shift his business to the economy where they get paid less. This may create more jobs for those people, theoretically raising their wages (but not in practice, at least not to the extent economists claim should happen). What happens is you've impoverished one economy without enriching the other. There is no good here. There is no upside for the worker. All that extra money remains in the hands of the owner. The factor that keeps this going is that for a while most of the first economy will remain intact, thus providing the illusion that this is a winning strategy. Until the economy crashes, that is."

The morality of free trade is at the heart of the debate over its effect on human rights and labor regulations, as is discussed by the authors of the viewpoints in the following chapter of *Opposing Viewpoints: Free Trade*. The authors examine many related issues, including social programs for workers who lose their jobs as a result of free trade agreements, the relative merits and challenges of labor unions, the proper role of government in ensuring the rights and safety of workers in free trade countries, and the effect of free trade on child labor.

"Society . . . owes all of its members . . . a level of protection against the unpredictable sufficient to afford them the opportunity to get back on their feet."

A Social Safety Net Is Needed for US Workers Displaced by Free Trade Agreements

R.A.

R.A. is a correspondent and blogger for the Economist. *In the following viewpoint, R.A. discusses economists' arguments over the relative value of liberalized (or "free") trade and offers commentary on these views. Protectionists' argument that people who lose their jobs due to free trade should be compensated is flawed, R.A. argues, because if businesses are never allowed to change practices, they cannot expand, which would be detrimental for both companies and society at large. Rather than side with protectionists, R.A. contends that he agrees with the economists who support free trade as well as support building social programs to assist people who become unemployed due to free trade.*

As you read, consider the following questions:

1. What does the viewpoint say is an uncomfortable truth for economists?

2. What does the author believe is often necessary following a policy change, in order to build sufficient support for that change?

3. What is the proper response to change that strikes the victims as unfair, according to R.A.?

The economics commentariat has been seized this week [in February 2011] with a debate over the value of trade liberalisation, of all things, sparked by a Greg Mankiw column in the *New York Times*, but really by Uwe Reinhardt's response to it, in which he cites Alan [S.] Blinder:

> "That is why I am going public with my concerns now," he concludes. "If we economists stubbornly insist on chanting 'free trade is good for you' to people who know that it is not, we will quickly become irrelevant to the public debate."

It's an uncomfortable truth for economists; perhaps all of whom have heard, at some point in their lives, the remark that "free trade is great in theory, but in practice . . .". Mark Thoma muses on the question and observes that just because trade *can* make everyone better off doesn't mean that it will. Trade liberalisation generally produces net benefits, such that some of the winners' gains can be redistributed to losers, leaving all in better shape than before. But this is not how policy functions in the real world. Should we support free trade if its Pareto [Pareto principle: 80 percent of the effect comes from 20 percent of the cause] improvements aren't actually realised?

Tim Worstall responds that the same argument can be made in reverse—the parties that benefit from protectionism never compensate those that lose from the restrictions. Since optimal redistribution is lacking in both cases, the most efficient solution should be the one we support: free trade.

In Support of Protectionism

William Polley is not happy with this conclusion:

> But ultimately what is wrong with Worstall's logic? For me, it boils down to the notion of a social contract. People make decisions, many of which are irrevocable or nearly so, on the basis of the best information and their expectations of the future. Sometimes the biggest influences on our expectations are the existing law and the political environment. If I then make a decision in good faith based on existing law, only to have the law change to my disadvantage, I will feel wronged. That I benefited from the way the law was should not be held against me when arguing to change the law. . . .
>
> And that's why Worstall's logic fails the test of reality. People make life decisions based on protectionism. No, not directly just like that. But trade protection has kept the factory in their hometown going. They graduate from high school and apply for a job. Maybe it was the only job in their hometown. Sure, they could have gone to the big city to wait on tables or drive a cab but that would take them away from home and family. They made the decision that was best for them based on what they knew and could in good faith expect. . . .
>
> When you break a contract in law, you must compensate the other party. Sometimes it is in the best interest of both parties to allow that. The social contract is no different. We can, and indeed we should, at times rewrite the social contract, but when we do, the winners must compensate those who made good faith decisions based on the old contract. If we do not, then the law is worth no more than the paper it is printed on, and that will lead to less economic activity for fear that it can always be taken away with the stroke of a pen.

I can see how this logic appeals to people, but it seems dead wrong to me. I believe in the social contract, and so I'm bothered by this attempt to redefine it as the whole of the existing body of law and regulation, and perhaps custom as well. Laws change. This is a fact of life and has been true for as long as there have been laws. People make important decisions on the basis of laws, and that's a reason to choose laws carefully, but it's also a reason to *make decisions* carefully. As a matter of political economy, it is often necessary to compensate the losers from a policy change in order to build sufficient support for that policy change. But that's a reason to oppose the recasting of the social contract in this way. To define the state's (or society's) obligations in this way—to say that current law at the time an individual makes critical decisions about the future (which is all the time) constitutes a contractual promise to that individual—is to make the status quo all but unchangeable. And in that, you do no one any favours.

In Support of Socially Responsible Free Trade

The best responses to Mr Polley's point that I've seen are this:

> I prefer to argue in favor of free trade because I think the right to choose who I wish to deal with belongs to me and your right to choose who you deal with belongs to you. I think, ultimately, government policies respecting these rights will promote economic growth and development, but that is mostly just a happy coincidence.

And this:

> I see the problem of adequately compensating the losers from international trade as just a part of the larger question of how we treat people in our society who, through no fault of their own, have fallen on hard times. International trade is just one of the many enormous, inexorable forces that constantly reshape our economy. Technological change, demographic change, or the fluctuations of the macroeconomic business cycle may devastate millions of families each year just as surely as international trade. An important mea-

sure (to me) of the type of society we live in is how we treat those individuals who are on the losing end of those impersonal economic forces that, in the long run, often help to make the world a more prosperous place.

Much of this conversation has centred around what economists can convincingly argue to a class of Rust Belt [heavily industrialised region of the United States] students in first-year economics. I'd tell them that economies are based on the gains from voluntary, mutually beneficial transactions, and the government should be very reluctant to prevent people from engaging in these transactions. No one wants to be told what or from which people they can buy. But what's price to one person is income to another. Sometimes people begin buying different things, for many different reasons—technological changes, policy changes, shifts in tastes, recessions—and that change in buying patterns will cost some people their income. Very often, these changes will strike the victim as unfair. But life, as parents have explained for millennia, is not fair. The proper response to this unfairness is not to try and undo it, to reject the choices of others engaging in voluntary transactions as illegitimate. The proper response is to work to build society's safety net so that those hit by life's inevitable unfairness aren't left destitute and hopeless because of it.

Society doesn't owe anyone a factory job, and it doesn't owe factory workers a cheque if an improvement in trade rules leaves them jobless. It owes them precisely what it owes all of its members: a level of protection against the unpredictable sufficient to afford them the opportunity to get back on their feet.

> *"Since the enactment of the North American Free Trade Agreement in 1994, the federal government's adoption of 'free trade' plans has produced 4.9 million job losses and the closure of some 43,000 factories."*

Obama's Free-Trade Victory Threatens 2012 Prospects

Roger Bybee

Roger Bybee is a Milwaukee-based freelance writer. In the following viewpoint, Bybee argues that since the enactment of the North American Free Trade Agreement (NAFTA), free trade plans have led to the loss of 4.9 million jobs. Anxieties about job losses and workers' rights are prevalent among the American people. The author contends that the South Korea free trade agreement is the most momentous in terms of American job losses. Bybee believes that by passing agreements with South Korea, Panama, and Colombia, President Barack Obama is promoting the loss of US jobs.

As you read, consider the following questions:

1. According to the viewpoint, what percentage of Democrats voted against the Colombia FTA?

2. Since 1994, the adoption of free trade plans has caused the closure of how many factories, according to Global Trade Watch?

3. As stated in the viewpoint, the Economic Policy Institute has projected how many job losses as a result of the South Korea deal?

By orchestrating the passage of three NAFTA [North American Free Trade Agreement]–style investor-rights agreements with South Korea, Colombia, and Panama, which passed Congress last week [in October 2011], President Barack Obama is promoting the loss of more U.S. jobs to low-wage sites overseas. He's also protecting Panama's status as a tax haven for U.S. corporations and money-laundering center for drug traffickers, leaving untouched the Colombian elite's murderous war against unionists and opening up U.S. laws and regulations to challenges from foreign corporations.

Moreover, by successfully pushing for the free trade deals, President Obama further reinforced the belief of many voters that Democratic leaders cannot be trusted in the fight to protect America's productive base against the forces of corporate globalization. He says he's focused on combating the flow of U.S. jobs to low-wage, high-repression nations, but the president's reversal in backing the three agreements follows the path trod by previous Democratic presidential candidates Bill Clinton and John Kerry, who both condemned free trade policies on the campaign trail and then supported them in practice.

Candidate Obama in 2008 was able to win the Democratic nomination and then the presidency only by waging a ferocious attack on the economic and social devastation caused by "free trade." In a typical speech, Obama thundered that

> decades of trade deals like NAFTA and China have been
> signed with plenty of protections for corporations and their
> profits, but none for our environment or our workers who've
> seen factories shut their doors and millions of jobs disap-
> pear; workers whose right to organize and unionize has
> been under assault for the last eight years.

Such rhetoric enabled Obama to carry crucial industrial states against John McCain in 2008. But following in the footsteps of Democratic president Bill Clinton, who promised tough "side agreements" to NAFTA to protect labor rights and environmental conditions in Mexico and 2004 Democratic presidential candidate John Kerry, who memorably railed against "Benedict Arnold CEOs" who moved jobs abroad, Obama has reversed course and embraced the agenda of Corporate America.

Clinton's much-touted "side agreements" turned out to be virtually toothless, but he never even dared to invoke these provisions in the face of incessant violations within Mexico. In 2004, candidate Kerry dropped the anti–"Benedict Arnold CEO" rhetoric once his nomination was assured. He has since returned to his embrace of "free trade."

Obama has furthered this pattern of betrayal by forcefully pushing for the three new "free trade" agreements. Aware of the antiglobalization sentiments of their economically squeezed constituents, "More Democratic congresspeople voted against President Obama's position than on any other issue," notes Todd Tucker, research director for Global Trade Watch.

Over 82 percent of Democrats voted against the Colombia FTA [free trade agreement], more than two-thirds stood against the Korea FTA and just over 64 percent opposed the Panama FTA. "Clearly, congresspeople understood what the right position was and where their core constituencies were on these agreements," Tucker says.

Anxieties Grow as "Free Trade" Results Become Clearer

Since the enactment of the North American Free Trade Agreement in 1994, the federal government's adoption of "free trade" plans has produced 4.9 million job losses and the closure of some 43,000 factories, according to Global Trade Watch.

Public alarm about "free trade" and the loss of American jobs was heightened when the *Wall Street Journal* reported April 2 that major U.S. firms had destroyed 2.9 million jobs at home and increased employment outside the U.S. by 2.4 million jobs since 2000.

Anxiety about the impact of job relocation to foreign sites is widespread among all political persuasions and income groups, with a fall 2010 *Wall Street Journal*/NBC poll showing that 86 percent of Americans "agreed that outsourcing of manufacturing to foreign countries with lower wages was a reason the U.S. economy was struggling and more people weren't being hired; no other factor was so often cited for current economic ills."

But Obama sidestepped this issue while campaigning for Democratic candidates in 2010 and thus forfeited the potential for credibly handing corporations a large share of the blame for persistent unemployment and widespread misery. With Obama rejecting the advice of Democratic advisors urging that the "offshoring" of U.S. jobs be highlighted, the 2010 midterm elections produced an unprecedented loss of 63 Democratic House seats and 6 among Senate Democrats.

Reflecting the public hostility toward "free trade," the current class of Democrats overwhelmingly rejected Obama's appeal to join him in backing the three deals. The *New York Times* quoted U.S. Rep. [Mike] Michaud of Maine: "What I am seeing firsthand is devastation that these free trade agreements can do to our communities."

Relying on Votes of Anti-Worker Republicans

In the House, the White House had to rely heavily on the votes of Republicans. Democrats like Michaud and many others expressed their fury at more trade agreements that will cost American jobs at a time of massive unemployment and undermine global standards for democracy and environmental protections.

The hoped-for alliance of progressive Democrats and non–Wall Street Republicans critical of corporate globalization largely evaporated into thin air. Tea Party–connected Republicans, although often portrayed in the mainstream media as "populists" angered both by Wall Street machinations and government "intrusion," have clearly shown their allegiance to Corporate America.

As a Global Trade Watch release observed, "Countless House Tea Party candidates ran paid ads attacking job offshoring, helping them make key inroads among working-class voters." But while using this posture to gain votes, ". . . virtually the entirety of the Tea Party–backed candidates sided with the president for job-offshoring deals," noted Global Trade Watch.

While the original Boston Tea Party of 1773 was a guerrilla action against the globalist East India Tea Company, as Thomas Hartmann points out in *Unequal Protection[: The Rise of Corporate Dominance and the Theft of Human Rights]*, the Tea Partiers in Congress appear instead firmly lined with the global corporations.

Unwilling to Change Fatal Footnote

Democratic congressional dissent was particularly sharp on the deal with Colombia, where between 2,800 and 4,000 unionists have been killed since 1986. During the 2008 campaign, Obama had stated that he would oppose the Colombia deal "because the violence against unions in Colombia would make a mockery of the very labor protections that we have insisted be included in these kinds of agreements."

Yet according to Tucker, the Obama administration consciously decided to make labor protections meaningless and unenforceable. Tucker explained:

> George W. Bush in 2007 changed these proposed trade agreement to include greater reference to international labor standards in the core text of agreements. But then Bush eviscerated these standards with a footnote excluding reference to ILO [International Labor Organization] labor standards [which would have been enforceable].

Labor organizations assumed that it would be an easy task to get the Obama administration to delete the fatal footnote. But the administration refused, Tucker told *In These Times*.

Even with intensified scrutiny of government and closely affiliated right-wing paramilitary groups, murders actually increased and barely any are prosecuted. "Ninety-seven percent of the past murders remain unprosecuted," stated Lori Wallach, director of Global Trade Watch. "Last month, a group of six leading human and labor rights advocates in Congress submitted a document noting that the conditions in Colombia made considering any trade agreement unacceptable and setting forth some real benchmarks for improvement.

"Obviously, if the goal of this administration action was to actually address the conditions in Colombia—where the number of unionist assassinations has grown during the period of maximum congressional and public scrutiny, from 37 when the FTA was signed in 2007 to 51 in 2010—a very different approach would be undertaken," Wallach says.

Promoting Labor Rights Within Trade Policies Makes Economic Sense

The United States for decades now has racked up large and growing trade deficits with the rest of the world. These deficits ... could contribute to much lower U.S. living standards in the future....

But what should policy makers do about it? One important approach is to increase the competitiveness of U.S. producers by investing in innovation here at home. Another is to promote the creation of a global middle class that can buy more high-end U.S. goods and services.... An integral part of this virtuous circle strategy is the promotion of enforceable labor rights, including by negotiating them as part of trade agreements.

Better labor standards in trading-partner countries, especially in less industrialized economies, can positively affect U.S. exports and U.S. imports. Better labor rights could increase demand for U.S. exports by boosting the incomes of workers overseas. And better labor standards abroad reduce the cost advantage that some countries may enjoy by paying their workers poorly....

Labor rights clearly have a positive effect on U.S. trade deficits, and thus help to put U.S. economic growth on a more durable path. Consequently, the promotion of labor standards, alongside environmental protections, should be an integral part of the future U.S. trade agenda.... The inclusion of labor rights in trade agreements with newly industrializing economies would result in higher U.S. exports and a growing global middle class.

Christian E. Weller and Stephen Zucconi,
"Labor Rights Can Be Good Policy: An Analysis of
US Trade with Less Industrialized Economies
with Weak or Strong Labor Rights,"
Center for American Progress, September 2008.

South Korea: Opening Funnel to Repressive Regimes' Production

The South Korea deal (known to Washington insiders as KO-RUS [FTA]) figures to be the most momentous in terms of job loss. The Economic Policy Institute has projected job losses of 159,000 and an increase in the U.S. trade deficit with Korea. Further, unionists see the deal as opening the door to components produced under atrocious conditions in North Korea and China, as I reported in June:

> "It is way worse than NAFTA," declares Matt McKinnon, political director of the International Association of Machinists and Aerospace Workers. All but two major unions oppose KORUS, and the AFL-CIO as a whole has been forceful in fighting the deal. "KORUS will be setting up a funnel for the worst actors in the region to get their products into the US under the South Korean label," McKinnon argues. It "will essentially be a regional trade deal under which we won't be able to exert any influence over the conditions in which the goods are produced."
>
> He explains that KORUS defines "South Korean–made" as any product that has at least 35% of its value created in South Korea. Under this rule, the origin of the remaining 65% does not matter.
>
> KORUS would potentially open up the United States to components produced under one of the world's most tightly repressive nations. The rigid police state of North Korea has opened up a free-trade zone employing about 40,000 workers currently. South Korean firms operating factories in the zone typically pay the North Korean government just $3 to $4 per day per worker, of which the worker gets to keep just $1.

Panama: Green Light to Tax Haven and Money-Laundering Center

Turning to the Panama trade deal, the agreement will leave in place Panama's ability to function as a center for tax evasion by U.S.-based corporations and wealthy citizens, as well as money laundering for narco-traffickers, said Global Trade Watch's Tucker.

A Citizens Trade Campaign paper on Panama warned of another major danger to U.S. efforts to regulate Wall Street and conduct of U.S. corporations: Panama is home to approximately 400,000 multinational subsidiaries, second in the world only to Hong Kong. Each one of those companies would be granted new powers under the new agreement's investment provisions to challenge new Panamanian or American financial oversight measures adopted in the future.

Obama's crucial support for the three "free trade" deals comes at a moment when a significant part of the potential Democratic base is literally marching in the opposite direction. The ongoing Occupy Wall Street [OWS] protests have the support of 54 percent of the American people, according to a recent poll.

In many respects, the multi-constituency, multi-issue protests have descended from the antiglobalization movement. Noted author of the book *The Shock Doctrine[: The Rise of Disaster Capitalism]* Naomi Klein said in her speech at Occupy Wall Street, "There is a direct connection between the messaging, energy and even many of the individuals involved in #OWS and the antiglobalization movement of the 1990s."

But Obama's response, according to Wallach, was to display his pro-business credentials by continuing the push for three new trade agreements. By upsetting much of the president's base, she argues, the prospects for Obama and Democratic House and Senate candidates in 2012 just grew dimmer:

> once again the administration's response to a GOP [Republican Party]/corporate hostage situation has been to betray its commitments and stomp its political base to comply with hostage takers whose goal is Democrats' defeat.

"New technologies and expanding global trade are weakening union attempts to maintain job cartels. Unions are driving investment and jobs away from the industries and states where they predominate."

US Labor Unions Interfere with Job Growth in a Free Trade Economy

James Sherk

James Sherk is senior policy analyst in labor economics at the Heritage Foundation. In the following viewpoint, Sherk discusses the influence of US unions on business, characterizing them as "job cartels" that protect the rights of a small percentage of workers at the expense of other workers and the economy at large. Sherk asserts that union control over the auto industry rendered Detroit automakers unable to compete with foreign automakers by driving up labor costs. In general, Sherk maintains, unions hamper companies' abilities to create jobs by restricting their labor pools and increasing their overheads, and restrict job growth by reducing the amount of money companies have avail-

able to invest and grow. Free trade and competitive markets, as well as technological advances, Sherk concludes, have made unions less powerful and increasingly unpopular with consumers and businesses.

As you read, consider the following questions:

1. According to the viewpoint, how much were automakers' labor costs in 2008?

2. According to the viewpoint, what percentage of the US economy were the values of imports in 1975 and 2011?

3. According to the viewpoint, by how much does employment drop after unions organize a business?

Everyone knows that unions try to raise their members' wages. But far fewer people understand how they try to do it. Unions cannot simply demand that companies hire their members for above-market wages. Employers would raise their eyebrows and simply say no.

To raise their members' pay, unions must control the supply of jobs in a company or an industry. Unions must prevent employers from hiring anyone without their permission. If they can do this, they can expect the laws of supply and demand to work in their favor. Holding down employment drives up union members' wages. In other words, successful unions are job cartels [trusts formed to regulate prices and control output].

The National Labor Relations Act (NLRA) gives unions this power. When a union "organizes" a company it obtains a monopoly over its jobs. The law authorizes a single union to act as the "exclusive bargaining representative" for employees in dealing with their employer. Businesses cannot directly hire workers. Instead they must first come to an agreement with the union over how many workers to hire and what to pay them. The monopoly gives the union the power to raise the wages of the company's employees.

For decades, the Detroit auto industry offered a model for demonstrating the power of a union cartel in action. By the early 1940s, the United Auto Workers (UAW) union had organized the Big Three automakers—General Motors, Ford, and Chrysler. The companies could not hire employees except on terms specified by the union.

Under the leadership of UAW president Walter Reuther, the UAW insisted on very generous compensation at each company. Reuther engaged in "pattern bargaining"—targeting one of the Big Three during contract negotiations for terms of a new (and usually generous) contract.

If the automaker would not pay, the union would strike, shutting down operations, sending business to the other two companies, and costing the targeted firm billions. So the target company routinely conceded to union demands. Reuther forced the other two automakers to accept contracts with similar terms. This strategy allowed the UAW to raise labor costs across the Big Three without putting any of the automakers out of business.

This arrangement worked incredibly well for UAW members. Until the automakers were forced into bankruptcy proceedings in 2008, their labor costs (wages and benefits) exceeded $70 an hour. UAW members enjoyed seven weeks of paid vacation and they could retire to generous pension benefits after 30 years on the job, irrespective of age. They earned more than many Ph.D. scientists.

However, the UAW—like all cartels—helped its members at the expense of the rest of the economy. Detroit automakers passed along the cost of inefficient work rules and higher labor costs by raising their prices. Since the Big Three controlled almost the entire U.S. market for cars, and since Reuther did not allow them to compete on labor costs, American consumers had little choice but to pay more for their product. That meant higher monthly car payments and less money to spend elsewhere. For some people, the higher costs made buying a car unaffordable. So Detroit built and sold fewer cars—and needed to hire fewer workers. The UAW raised its members' wages by raising prices and by restricting the job opportunities for everyone else.

The Power of Competition

For many years, this was the pattern of auto industry employment and wages. But what eventually happened to Detroit automakers demonstrates the limits of union power. After General Motors and Chrysler filed for bankruptcy, they negotiated new contracts that substantially reduced their labor costs. And despite promises of job security, many UAW members lost their jobs.

What happened? Competition.

The UAW lost its control over the supply of jobs in the auto industry. In the late 1970s, foreign automakers entered the U.S. auto market. In many cases, they did not make "foreign cars." Instead, they produced vehicles built by American workers in the United States—but built by nonunion workers in southern states. Consumers could now choose whether or not to buy cars made by UAW members who worked for automakers headquartered in Detroit.

This competition hugely benefited the economy. Consumers decided that foreign automakers transplanted to America were making cars of higher quality and lower cost than Detroit's. To stay competitive, Detroit automakers had to cut their costs and increase their quality. When that began to happen, every American outside the UAW who purchased a car was better off.

But Detroit's response to the new competition was insufficient. Americans voted with their wallets and the Big Three's market share shrank. By 2007 Detroit automakers were producing less than half the vehicles sold in the United States. By 2008 their financial position had so deteriorated that the recession pushed General Motors and Chrysler into bankruptcy.

As a result, labor costs in the new UAW contracts are now little higher than what nonunion autoworkers make.

Competition works to prevent cartels from benefiting their members or damaging the economy. If consumers have non-union choices, then unionized firms cannot pass their higher costs on to them. Only if unions can restrict competition for jobs can they benefit union members.

How Unions Restrict Competition for Labor

An incident last September [in 2011] in Washington State illustrates the importance unions attach to restricting competition for jobs. In a scene that could have come from the 1954 movie *On the Waterfront* the Associated Press reported, "Hundreds of angry longshoremen stormed through a grain shipping terminal in Longview, Wash., early Thursday and held security guards at bay while descending on a disputed train full of grain, cutting brake lines and dumping cargo."

The International Longshore and Warehouse Union (ILWU) attacked the terminal to prevent another union from competing with it for dock work. The ILWU had previously organized every port on the West Coast. And it used its monopoly on dock labor to drive up the average wages of its member employees to $125,000 a year, plus $80,000 in benefits.

An employer called EGT Development built a grain terminal at the Port of Longview and hired workers from a different union to run it. This gave farmers a port from which to ship their grain without paying ILWU members $200,000 a year.

The ILWU didn't want farmers to have that choice. So its members overpowered guards, threw out grain, and sabotaged trains. The union tried to physically prevent other American workers from competing with it.

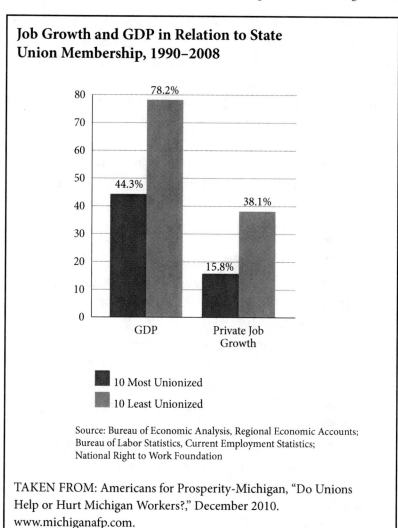

Job Growth and GDP in Relation to State Union Membership, 1990–2008

Source: Bureau of Economic Analysis, Regional Economic Accounts;
Bureau of Labor Statistics, Current Employment Statistics;
National Right to Work Foundation

TAKEN FROM: Americans for Prosperity-Michigan, "Do Unions Help or Hurt Michigan Workers?," December 2010. www.michiganafp.com.

How Unions Use Government's Monopoly Powers

In this case, the union overstepped a boundary because there are laws against violence and a judge quickly issued an injunction against the ILWU. More typically, however, unions today use government to restrict competition for them.

Unions lobby for government trade barriers that prevent Americans from buying from foreign competitors. They campaign for project labor agreements that force construction contractors to sign collective bargaining agreements before beginning work. They take full advantage of the government rules and mandates by using regulations to shut down competitors.

For example, a few years ago Ausra [Inc.] applied to build a solar power plant in the California desert. Most environmentalists consider solar power a "green" energy source. Nonetheless a coalition of construction unions called California Unions for Reliable Energy (or CURE), demanded that Ausra first study the project's effect on the short-nosed kangaroo rat and the ferruginous hawk. These environmental impact assessments tied up the company with delays and prevented the project from moving forward.

One of Ausra's competitors, BrightSource Energy, also applied to build a solar plant in California. This project was larger and it would affect the habitat of the imperiled desert tortoise. But this time, CURE urged regulators to approve the application as quickly as possible.

What made the difference? BrightSource agreed to hire only union workers on its project while Ausra refused to sign a similar deal. The union used environmental lawsuits to tie up Ausra in green tape. That's one way a union can use government regulations to freeze out nonunion competition.

More Competition and Freer Markets Make a Difference

Fortunately for consumers, but unfortunately for unions, the American economy has become much more competitive over the past generation. Both Republican and Democratic administrations have deregulated parts of the economy. President [Jimmy] Carter deregulated the trucking industry, while President [Ronald] Reagan's Justice Department broke up the Bell [telephone services] monopoly. And both Republican and Democratic administrations passed free trade deals that opened up American markets. In 1975 the value of imports amounted to 7.5 percent of the U.S. economy. By 2011 that figure had risen to 16 percent.

Technology has also increased the pressure of competition. In recent decades, transportation costs have fallen sharply thanks to improvements in supply chain technologies, which let out-of-state companies compete with local businesses. And the Internet makes it easy for consumers to compare prices and order from distant competitors.

These changes mean less expensive and higher quality products for Americans. They also make it very difficult for unions to prevent Americans from buying products made by nonunion workers. The union business model—designed during and immediately after the Great Depression—fits poorly into the modern competitive economy. As a result, unions can no longer deliver the same benefits to their members that they used to.

The Perverse Effect of Unions on Wages

Unions like to point to studies that compare the pay of union and nonunion workers. After controlling for other factors—education, experience, etc.—these studies typically find that union members earn 20 percent more than comparable nonunion employees. But economists have exhaustively examined the effects unions have on wages, and have discovered one surprising finding: Unions cannot take most of the credit for these higher wages. For many employees, being a member of a union no longer delivers a substantial wage premium.

How can this be, since union members do earn more? The answer is that unions are not the reason their members have higher wages. Union contracts make it difficult to lay off unproductive employees. As a result, unionized companies become very selective about whom they hire. Knowing they cannot get rid of bad apples, companies take more care to hire higher quality workers.

Research shows that more productive workers, whether unionized or not, earn higher wages—and this helps explain some union members' higher pay. In many of these cases, it's not that unions are responsible for negotiating higher pay for workers; it's that unionized companies have an incentive to pay more to hire and retain productive workers knowing that whomever they hire can't be easily fired. Economists have tracked the wages of individual workers as they join and leave unionized companies. This enables economists to account for higher unobserved individual productivity. These studies find a much smaller than expected union premium—only 8 to 12 percent.

A similar perverse effect can be found in how unions pick companies to organize. You might think that unions would try to organize small and weak companies. In fact, they target larger and more profitable companies for unionizing drives. Unions know that workers have little appetite for unionizing when their firm is unprofitable and on the brink of collapse. They are more likely to unionize if they believe their company has earnings to spare. The irony is that larger and more profitable companies tend to pay higher wages—with or without a union.

Several studies have compared workers at companies who vote to unionize with workers at similar companies that vote against unionizing. They come to the surprising conclusion that—at these companies at least—unionizing did not raise pay. This does not prove that union cartels do not raise wages. But it does show that in today's competitive economy, unions do not raise pay nearly as much as they claim to. In some companies, unions don't raise pay at all.

Unions Reduce Corporate Investment

The companies where unions can raise pay are those that have a competitive advantage in the marketplace. Unions raise wages at companies that are sheltered from foreign competition or those with a growing demand for their product. Unions can also redistribute profits away from a company's research and development [R&D] projects or long-term investments to unionized employees. The companies that can afford to grant union pay demands are those that have less fear of losing business.

Try this thought experiment. Imagine if General Motors had invested heavily in R&D and invented an inexpensive hybrid car that got 150 miles to the gallon. The company's sales and profits would soar. Toyota or Honda would not be able to produce comparable vehicles. How would the UAW react?

Instead of making concessions that lowered their members' compensation to nonunion rates, which is what happened when Detroit automakers were driven to bankruptcy, the UAW would be demanding even higher pay. Union officials would want their members to make $100 an hour instead of $70. In essence, unions seek to tax the profits of successful investments. If the investments pan out, then unions demand that a part of the profits go to their members. But this reduces the return on investing for unionized companies.

Businesses respond to union "taxes" in the same way that they respond to government taxes: They invest less. Studies show that unionized companies invest about 15 percent less in both physical capital and R&D than comparable nonunion companies. Research shows that unions directly cause this reduction; it is not just a correlation. Investment falls at companies after unions organize them. One study found that being unionized has the same effect on business investment as a 33 percentage increase in the corporate income tax. Less investment makes businesses less competitive.

Unions Reduce Companies' Flexibility and Competitiveness

Unions have a harmful effect on business efficiency in other ways. Collective bargaining—by definition—prevents a company from dealing directly with its employees. Changes to working conditions must be negotiated through the union. Unions claim this arrangement gives employees an institutional "voice" to amplify their demands to management. However, it also prevents companies from treating their employees as individuals. One master contract covers all workers. One result is that at a unionized firm, seniority, not individual performance, dictates who gets a promotion or raise. Unionized firms cannot reward individual excellence.

Unions also reduce the flexibility of the companies they organize. Unionized employers cannot respond to competitive pressures by immediately changing their business plan. They must first negotiate with their unions. Contract negotiations can take many months and cost hundreds of thousands of dollars in legal fees. Unions often insist on concessions in exchange for new contract provisions. The upshot is that unionized businesses often try to avoid making changes because they are not worth the cost or time spent at the bargaining table. This sluggishness makes unionized businesses less competitive. They cannot respond as rapidly or flexibly as their unorganized competitors.

Unionized Companies Create Fewer Jobs

If unionized companies are less flexible and invest less than nonunion companies, then we would expect them to grow more slowly and create fewer jobs. Unsurprisingly, research shows that this is exactly what happens. Employment drops 5 to 10 percent after unions organize a business. Thereafter, jobs in unionized companies grow more slowly (or shrink more rapidly) by an average of about 3 to 4 percentage points than at comparable nonunion companies. Of course unions try to avoid pushing the businesses they organize over a cliff. Research shows that unionized companies do not go out of business at higher rates than nonunion firms. Nonetheless, unions accept slower growth and gradual job losses as the price they are willing to pay for the contract provisions they want for their existing members.

If union members really wanted to help their employer succeed, it's conceivable that they could decide not to "tax" away its profits at the bargaining table. That would encourage unionized companies to invest more and create more jobs. But given a choice between demanding higher pay for current union members or creating more company jobs in the future, unions usually pick higher pay.

Similarly, one can imagine that unions might negotiate very broad "management rights" clauses allowing businesses the flexibility to respond to changing business conditions without going back to the bargaining table. But it's clear that most unions prefer to exercise as much veto power as possible over a firm's employment decisions. At unionized firms, layoffs occur on the basis of seniority, so the most senior union members know they are least likely to lose their jobs if the company gets in trouble. Most union members (who are not new hires) prefer layoffs.

Unions typically choose not to accept the changes necessary to prevent unionized companies from shrinking in a competitive economy. . . .

Unions Must Adapt to Modern Technology and Trade Realities

What unions do has hardly changed since the end of World War II. They still try to organize workers and win pay increases and benefits for their members by controlling the supply of jobs at a company or in an industry.

But while the union movement insists on using traditional methods to organize workers and negotiate with employers, the American economy and workforce is undergoing very dramatic changes. New technologies and expanding global trade are weakening union attempts to maintain job cartels. Unions are driving investment and jobs away from the industries and states where they predominate.

The union movement has to develop a new model for doing business. If it can't or won't, the answer to the question "What do unions do?" will soon be: "Not much."

> "For the unionists struggling for survival, an imbalanced trade deal would further compound the power imbalance in Colombia's labor system, where the price a worker pays for raising his voice is meted out in blood."

Free Trade Agreements Threaten the Lives of Labor Activists in Developing Countries

Michelle Chen

Michelle Chen is a contributing editor at In These Times. *In the following viewpoint, Chen describes the risks that Colombian activists take when speaking out against a possible free trade agreement between the United States and Colombia. These activists, Chen reports, want the United States to terminate any business agreements with a country where speaking out for labor rights can be a death sentence. According to Chen, the Barack Obama administration's labor action plan, intended to rein in violence and rights abuses, has failed to convince activists that it is adequate because it lacks key provisions and means of enforcement.*

Chen reports that violence against trade unionists is only one of many problems Colombia faces, including its ongoing drug war and internal ethnic and political conflicts, and that current strategies to address these problems do not reflect the stark realities of Colombian trade unionists' lives.

As you read, consider the following questions:

1. What company is "a notorious union buster at home and abroad," according to the viewpoint?

2. What is the fundamental limitation of the labor action plan (LAP), according to Carlos Olaya, as quoted in the viewpoint?

3. How many trade unionists were murdered in Colombia in 2010, according to the viewpoint?

Gathering with fellow unionists in Washington, D.C., Jose Hugo Yanini speaks firmly about labor rights in Colombia. But a few weeks ago, the industrial janitor and shop steward feared that he soon might never utter another word.

Yanini, who is campaigning with SEIU [Service Employees International Union] and other groups against the pending U.S.-Colombia trade agreement, is a typical target in his home country. Last month [June 2011], on his way home from collective bargaining talks, labor activists report, he got the anonymous phone message that every Colombian union activist dreads: "Tell that man that he should be careful with his tongue or we will cut it out."

So far, the case hasn't been fully investigated and the public doesn't know who was behind the menacing call. But people do know Yanini's boss: the multinational company Sodexo, a major provider of food and custodial services in the U.S. and other countries, and a notorious union buster at home and abroad.

What brought Yanini and other Colombian unionists to Washington is a simple demand that the U.S. simply not continue to do business with a country where speaking out for labor rights can be a death sentence.

The Colombia Free Trade Agreement Heightens Dangers

The Colombia free trade agreement [FTA] has been pending for years in Congress along with other trade deals, stalled by political stalemate as well as intense opposition by unions and human rights advocates. It would strip away tariffs and, like the North American Free Trade Agreement [NAFTA], subject both countries to a series of byzantine bilateral trade rules ostensibly designed to maximize profit. In reality, as with NAFTA, the deal is designed to maximize exploitation and minimize corporate and government accountability.

Earlier this year, the [Barack] Obama administration touted the labor action plan [LAP], a joint agreement to enhance labor laws and regulatory mechanisms. Though the plan contains provisions that look good on paper—such as legal reforms to bar certain labor abuses and antiunion activities—advocates fear that it's just window dressing for a deal designed to enrich the companies that keep workers impoverished and silenced.

According to U.S. Labor Education in the Americas Project (US LEAP), the LAP does meet some of the demands of labor unions by promising stronger enforcement of labor law and preventing employers from undermining organized labor by exploiting contract and cooperative systems. But in an April statement, the group concluded:

> (1) does not require an actual reduction in violence against trade unionists or advances on impunity, (2) is limited only to labor issues and does not address a wide range of other concerns, including human rights violations, militarization, impact on agriculture, internal displacement and the rights of Afro-Colombians, and (3) provides no way to ensure compliance once the Colombia FTA is implemented. Conse-

Violence Against Trade Unionists

Colombia still leads the world in killings of trade unionists, with more than 2,800 reported killings since 1986, according to the National Labor School (ENS), Colombia's leading NGO [nongovernmental organization] monitoring labor rights. Most are attributed to paramilitaries and their successor groups.

While the number of murders dropped in 2007 to 39, statistics are still alarmingly high: 52 murders in 2008, 47 in 2009, and 36 from January to September 15, 2010, according to the ENS. Threats against unionists—mostly attributed to paramilitaries' successor groups—have increased since 2007.

Human Rights Watch, "World Report 2011: Colombia," January 2011. www.hrw.org.

quently, prominent labor and human rights groups have joined leading Colombian trade union organizations in denouncing the agreement as woefully inadequate as a sufficient condition for approval of the FTA.

The Grim Reality of Workers' Lives

Colombian activists came to D.C. to give a ground-level perspective of the gap between the LAP's official language and the reality that workers face every day.

Carlos Olaya, director of research with the union SINALTRAINAL, is skeptical that the labor accord would alleviate obstacles to effective labor organizing.

Even organized workers have "no real access to collective bargaining rights," he said, recalling that in his union, negotiations with various companies fell apart and left workers "stuck in limbo." The fundamental limitation of the LAP, he said, is that:

it's not changing the business culture, which is one of indirect contracting and not hiring workers in a way that allows them to access their rights. And there's an ongoing anti-union culture.... It does not address those kinds of root problems, and so workers are continuing to lack access to their labor and human rights.

Beyond labor issues, Colombia suffers from a whole range of crises: a monstrous drug war, ongoing factional conflicts, and deep marginalization of Afro-Colombian and indigenous communities. All of these problems are interlocked in a climate of impunity and corruption, which is symbolized by Colombia's distinction as labor murder capital of the world.

In 2010 alone, according to US LEAP, 51 trade unionists were murdered—a considerable increase since 2007, when the Colombian Congress initially approved the pact. Between 2006 and 2010, a staggering 239 trade unionists were killed in Colombia, compared with 265 unionists killed in all other countries combined. The vast majority of cases documented over a quarter century have not resulted in convictions. In light of the vast inequities plaguing the Western Hemisphere, perhaps it's not so ironic that the country's chaos and oppression has paralleled relatively solid economic growth and plenty of aid from the U.S.

Washington's Standard Approach Is Not Enough

The standard Washington prescription for this social malaise would be more unfettered foreign trade in the name of economic uplift and social stability. But Yanini, whose outspokenness may have nearly cost him a body part, has a different take.

"I work at Sodexo. Sodexo is a very large multinational company that has very high earnings every year. And yet we as workers there have not benefited from anything because they have not wanted to give us any benefits," he said, adding that the company refused to accommodate health problems, including tendonitis, that limited his ability to work. "They fired seven of my colleagues that wanted to join our union," he recalled, "just because they wanted to join a union."

Repudiating the all-boats-rise rhetoric, he said, "that's a good example of how even large companies that have lots of money are not sharing that wealth with us as workers."

Though the labor action plan seems to reflect essential labor rights principles, it's embedded in a trade liberalization regime that undermines human rights and democracy. So the activists who oppose the Colombia FTA won't be satisfied with labor provisions that focus only on the workplace, without addressing other potential consequences for civil society, for agriculture communities and marginalized groups. By design, that kind of U.S.-Colombia trade "partnership" would simply reward injustice with foreign investment.

"The key issue here," Olaya said, "is that there's a large imbalance in that relationship between the U.S. and Colombia. In many ways, both with the FTA and otherwise, the U.S. has a lot of power to impose itself in Colombia."

For the unionists struggling for survival, an imbalanced trade deal would further compound the power imbalance in Colombia's labor system, where the price a worker pays for raising his voice is meted out in blood.

> *"International pressure led Ecuador, in 2005, to launch reforms to reduce child labor, but as of 2010, 13% of the country's children are still working, often in agriculture."*

Free Trade Agreements Have Failed to End the Exploitation of Child Laborers

Max Fisher

Max Fisher is an associate editor at the Atlantic. *In the following viewpoint, Fisher explains that while free trade agreements between the United States and Colombia have helped lower the incidence of child labor being used in the flower industry in that country, children in other parts of the world are still exploited. Fisher indicates that American consumers are largely unaware that their purchases are supporting child labor. He suggests that increased awareness and insistence on purchasing only fair trade–certified goods produced according to strict human rights standards could go a long way toward eliminating the problem, until further trade restrictions can be imposed in other countries.*

As you read, consider the following questions:

1. According to the author, how much do American adults spend (in billions of dollars) on the Valentine's Day fresh flower tradition?

2. What percentage of flowers bought in the United States on Valentine's Day were cut by child laborers in Ecuador, according to the viewpoint?

3. What American president gets the credit, according to Fisher, for helping to get children off of Colombia's flower plantations?

More than one in three American adults will buy flowers today [February 14, 2012], spending $1.7 billion dollars on this Valentine's Day tradition. The majority of those flowers will come from Colombia and Ecuador, two of the world's leading producers. But these countries, and their flowers industries specifically, have troubled records of abusing workers or hiring children, and your well-intentioned roses might go toward supporting some of these practices.

Because the flower industry is driven by human labor, when demand skyrockets around Valentine's Day, Colombian and Ecuadorian growers can't just open a valve to increase production. They have to get more labor out of their existing employees, sometimes having them work up to 20 hours a day, and they have to hire on new workers. Often, that means children.

At least 8.3% of flowers in the U.S. were cut by child laborers in Ecuador, or about one in 12 stems, according to the most recent data. During the school year, 80% of the workers in Ecuador's enormous flower industry are children, according to a 2000 report by the International Labour Organization. That's the most recent data specific to the flower industry, but it may not have changed much; international pressure led Ecuador, in 2005, to launch reforms to reduce child labor, but as of 2010, 13% of the country's children are still working, often in agriculture.

Far more of our flowers come from Colombia, where, according to the International Labor Rights Forum, "child labor has been successfully eradicated in Colombian flower plantations." Only a decade ago, an alarming State Department report on Colombia found that "children as young as 11 years of age work full-time in almost every aspect of the cut flower industry." Though child labor is still a significant problem in coffee and sugarcane, getting children off of Colombia's flower plantations was a real success. What happened?

Child Labor Numbers Have Decreased but Abuses Continue

Believe it or not, a significant share of the credit goes to George W. Bush. In 2006, his administration started working with Colombia on a free trade deal, but he made it about more than just trade. The deal would require that Colombia meet and enforce certain workers' rights standards, including on child labor. Colombia, which for years had resisted pressure to improve workers' conditions, happily agreed. And why not? A free trade would be so great for Colombia's economy that ending child labor, allowing stronger unions, and improving basic services were well worth the trade-off. Congress finally approved the deal last year [2011], and it is expected to go into effect by the end of 2012.

Still, even if the U.S. can push to end child labor on Ecuadorian flower plantations the way it did in Colombia, that won't make the industry much friendlier to its workers. Two-thirds of flower workers in both countries suffer from work-related health problems: mostly things like nausea or impaired vision, but sometimes asthma, birth defects, or even miscarriages. Labor rights organizations cite the industry's use of dangerous pesticides. The U.S. Labor Education in the Americas Project says that 20% of the pesticides are so toxic that they're either restricted or outright banned in the U.S. and Europe.

Women Also Suffer

Women in Ecuador, who make up half of the country's flower workforce, often face abusive conditions at plantations. Of the women interviewed by the International Labor Rights Forum in 2005, 55% said they'd been subject to sexual harassment at work and 19% that they'd been forced to have sex with a supervisor or coworker. This means that 5.7% of flowers you see for sale today were cut by women who'd been sexually harassed, and 2.0% cut by women who were forced to sleep with someone at work.

The conditions aren't as bad in Colombia, but women are routinely fired if they become pregnant. One NGO [nongovernmental organization] says that, every day, their office receives an average of two women who've lost their flower-cutting jobs after being discovered as pregnant.

A reality of our globalized economy is that rich countries buy lots of things from poor countries, and that poor countries tend to treat their workers a lot worse. That's not because poor countries need to abuse their workers in order to compete—practices like child labor are actually a net loss for the economy. It's because, among many other reasons, they tend to have weaker court systems and frail labor unions, meaning that workers have a harder time fighting abusive employers, and wages are often so low that hungry parents have little choice but to send their children to get jobs. Employers have little incentive to improve.

U.S. Consumers Can Help Curb the Use of Child Labor

Fortunately, the U.S. can help. American consumers have more power over flower plantation owners than maybe anybody on

Trade Sanctions and Poverty

One root cause of child labour is poverty—families with working children tend to be poor and often send some children to work in order to afford schooling for at least one or two of their children. If their income falls because of trade sanctions, these families may be forced to rely even more on child labour to make ends meet. So even if international action succeeds in moving children out of export industries, more children may end up working.

Matthias Doepke and Fabrizio Zilibotti,
"Child Labour: Is International Activism the Solution
or the Problem?," Vox, October 12, 2009. www.voxeu.org.

earth. If Americans refuse to buy from a plantation that uses child labor, they can shut it down overnight. The problem, of course, is how to tell the difference. Though more Americans are buying fair trade, most are either unaware of the difference, don't think to look for fair trade flowers, or just don't think about it. Rushing by the grocery store to buy some flowers for your spouse in time for dinner, you probably don't have the time or inclination to investigate their source.

When the U.S.-Colombia free trade agreement finally goes into effect later this year, it will make Colombian flowers cheaper, and Ecuadorian flowers more expensive by comparison. This means that more flower-cutting jobs will shift to Colombia, where there are still-not-great but improved labor standards as a result of the free trade deal.

In the short run, this is bad news for Ecuadorian flower cutters any way you look at it. They will have fewer jobs and employers could get even cheaper in a desperate effort to drive down their prices. But, in the long term, as long as the U.S. keeps using its collective buying power to promote workers' rights, Ecuador's industry may come to understand that competing for American dollars requires meeting labor standards. That's not just because U.S. consumers are more aware of the power their money has to either improve or worsen the lives of hardworking families thousands of miles away. It's also because, the more rights-promoting free trade agreements that Congress passes, the more that selling to America will require enforcing good labor standards. Ecuador and the U.S. actually began discussing just one such agreement in 2004, but negotiations collapsed in 2006; once Colombia starts outcompeting, Ecuadorian leaders may have to reconsider.

So there are reasons to believe that we're learning how to manage child labor out of the international flower market. But we're not there yet. Consumers are still a little too indifferent, and most of our trade has no Colombia-style labor rights requirements. Americans will still spend over a hundred million dollars on flowers cut by child laborers today, and they won't even know it.

> *"Free trade is a human right—not an absolute right, but a right that governments should only circumscribe in the most adverse of circumstances."*

Free Trade Is a Fundamental Human Right

Samuel Gregg

Samuel Gregg is research director at the Acton Institute. In the following viewpoint, Gregg explains why a decline in world trade during the current global economic downturn might severely exacerbate the crisis. Gregg provides extensive historical evidence that claims that free trade is a fundamental human right, citing Adam Smith's challenges to mercantilism in the eighteenth century as well as earlier treatises. These ideas, Gregg concludes, are just as relevant in the modern economy, in which protectionist trade restrictions unjustly limit the ability of many humans to exercise their right to engage in trade as well as utilize the entire range of available resources.

As you read, consider the following questions:

1. According to Gregg, by how much will the total world trade in goods and services decline in 2009?

2. What provisions of the 2009 US stimulus package passed by Congress actively discriminated against foreign imports, according to Gregg?

3. According to Gregg, what expectation on the part of Great Britain was "as absurd as to expect that an Oceana or Utopia should ever be established in it"?

In the wake of the high unemployment, mortgage foreclosures, and general economic uncertainty flowing from the financial crisis, most Americans have understandably focused on its domestic effects. Far less attention has been given to the global recession's international ramifications. This is unfortunate, for one of the most significant effects has been a profound decline in world trade—and this, in turn, may serve to exacerbate the crisis.

Estimates vary, but according to the IMF [International Monetary Fund] total world trade in goods and services will decline by 12.2% in 2009. Accompanying these developments have been fears of resurgent protectionism. The *Economist* argues, however, that such worries have proved to be overrated. In one sense, this is true. If by protectionism we mean the raising of tariff barriers, then we have not seen anything like the 1930 Smoot-Hawley Tariff Act that limited foreign access to America's markets and helped facilitate the Great Depression. Indeed, some countries, such as Australia and China, have actually reduced import duties.

On the other hand, the European Union and the United States have introduced new farm subsidies to already outrageously subsidized agricultural sectors. Moreover, there are other ways to impede or distort the relatively free access of individuals and businesses to global markets. One example is the early 2009 stimulus package passed by the American Congress. It contains "Buy American" provisions that actively discriminate against foreign imports.

Impediments to Free Trade Linked to Cap and Trade

Yet another instance of creeping impediments to free trade is the recent demand by several United States senators that any cap-and-trade bill contain "a longer-term border adjustment mechanism"—in other words, a tariff—to protect American industry against competition from countries that refuse to adopt expensive carbon-emission measures similar to those contained in the Waxman-Markey Bill [officially known as the American Clean Energy and Security Act] passed by the House of Representatives. Some European Union [EU] countries, most notably France, have insisted that "economic measures" should be taken against those countries that don't enact carbon-emission requirements like those embraced by the EU. India and China have already told the United States they have no intention of adopting such policies on the grounds that they would drastically impede these nations' ongoing rise out of poverty—one of the economic miracles of our time.

But why, some might ask, are these emerging barriers to free trade so worrying? Shouldn't governments encourage "economically patriotic" policies? Surely a government should "look after its own."

There are two reasons why free trade should be protected and promoted. The first concerns free trade's profound contribution to global economic prosperity. The second is that free trade is a human right—not an absolute right, but a right that governments should only circumscribe in the most adverse of circumstances.

Adam Smith and Free Trade

The economic case for free trade was codified by Adam Smith when his *Wealth of Nations* was published in 1776. He challenged the then reigning mercantilist orthodoxy that one country could only become richer at other nations' expense. "The modern maxims of foreign commerce," Smith wrote, "by

Free Trade Is a Matter of Free Will and Liberty

Free trade isn't a battle that countries (or states) win or lose. It is a human right—the liberty to engage in voluntary transactions that leave both participants better off.

Jeff Jacoby,
"The Old Delusion of Protectionism,"
Boston Globe, *January 10, 2010.*

aiming at the impoverishment of all our neighbors, so far as they are capable of producing their intended effect, tend to render that very commerce insignificant and contemptible." Observing the political and economic conflict between the eighteenth century's two great powers, France and Britain, Smith commented, "If those two countries . . . were to consider their real interest, without either mercantile jealously or national animosity, the commerce of France might be more advantageous to Great Britain . . . and for that same reason that of Great Britain to France."

Smith's point was simple yet revolutionary: Free trade would, in the long term, mutually enrich everyone. For one thing, free trade encouraged an ever-increasing depth and sophistication of the division of labor. This facilitated technological development and the ability to grow ever-increasing amounts of wealth. Free trade also created an ever-widening space for individuals, businesses, and entire nations to find, develop, or even change their comparative advantage. As Smith put it, "If a foreign country can supply us with a commodity cheaper than we ourselves can make it, better buy it of them with some part of the produce of our own industry employed in a way in which we have some advantage."

It was certainly possible, Smith noted, for a country like Scotland to grow grapes. The financial cost, however, of doing so compared to, for example, growing grapes in Italy, made that an economically foolish choice for Scots. By contrast, individuals, businesses, and countries in a global free market would be encouraged to focus on doing what they did best and would not be incentivized by protectionism into developing industries that, in the long run, couldn't compete in the marketplace, even with extensive tariffs.

Appeals to economic efficiency and prosperity are enough for some, but just as human beings are more than *homo economicus* (and Smith himself never thought that human life could be reduced to economics) so too are purely economic arguments insufficient for governments to adopt particular policies, even those concerning economic subjects. But if governments have some responsibility to protect their citizens' rights, then perhaps they may wish to consider the claim that the liberty to trade goods and services across national boundaries is not a privilege but rather a *right*.

Excessive rights-talk disfigures much contemporary political discussion, but compared to most modern rights-claims, the idea of free trade as a right has both a much older lineage and a more coherent rational basis. The first to apply the word "right" to free trade was the sixteenth-century scholar Francisco de Vitoria (1492–1546) in his *De Indis et de Ivre Belli Relectiones* (1532).

According to Vitoria, the right to free trade was derived from the natural right of free association enjoyed by all people. Free association, to Vitoria's mind, was essential for human flourishing, and he did not believe national boundaries should unreasonably limit people from freely associating with others, including for economic reasons. Interestingly, Vitoria developed this line of argument in the context of claiming that the New World's native peoples should not be prevented from freely trading with European merchants by either their indigenous rulers or European monarchs. Such were Vitoria's convictions against mercantilist policies that he even depicted laws unduly limiting free trade between nations as "iniquitous and against charity."

The Dutch philosopher and jurist Hugo Grotius (1583–1645) also built a rights-based case for free trade. As a target, Grotius aimed at the Portuguese claim to a monopoly of the trade routes to the East Indies. In *Mare Liberum* (1609), Grotius employed uncharacteristically insistent language to maintain, as an "unimpeachable axiom of the Law of Nations . . . the spirit of which is self-evident and immutable," that "every nation is free to travel to every other nation, and to trade with it."

Grotius's argument for free trade as a right was based on the premise that nature did not supply every place with the necessities of life. Moreover, Grotius observed (foreshadowing Smith's economic analysis) that it was clear that "some nations excel in one art and others in another." These factors meant that if the goods of the world were truly to serve everyone, then free trade was a necessity. Grotius notes that his argument was hardly novel, as it could be found in the works of Roman philosophers such as Seneca (4 B.C.–65 A.D.). Almost a century after Grotius's death, we find the same position stated in the most important eighteenth-century text on international law, Emer de Vattel's *Le droit de gens* (1758). This book insists that the "obligation," as Vattel describes it, of nations to engage in mutual commerce, means that those "privileges and tolls, which obtain in many places, and press so heavily upon commerce, are deservedly to be reprobated."

To be sure, none of these thinkers considered free trade to be an absolute right. Grotius and Vattel believed, for example, that states engaged in a legitimate war could justly prohibit its citizens from trading with citizens of enemy powers. Nor was Smith an absolutist about free trade. In some circumstances, he was willing to approve certain subsidies for particular industries. Generally, however, Smith insisted that the onus of proof for the wisdom of interfering with free trade lay with those proposing a restriction or subsidy.

Will free trade, either as a right or an empirically validated economic argument, ever gain universal acceptance? Smith himself concluded there was so much resistance to free trade arising both from economic ignorance and also established interests determined to protect themselves from competition by whatever means necessary that "to expect . . . that freedom of trade should ever be entirely restored in Great Britain, is as absurd as to expect that an Oceana or Utopia should ever be established in it."

One of Smith's contemporaries and greatest admirers, the English philosopher and politician Edmund Burke, once wrote that "free trade is not based on utility but on justice." Certainly the economic argument for free trade's long-term economic utility and protectionism's detrimental effects is difficult to refute. Yet it may be that free trade's greatest hope in the long term will be that enough people recognize there is something fundamentally unjust about unduly impeding the ability of all the world's resources to serve all human beings in an increasingly globalized world in which nation-state borders mean less and less.

Periodical and Internet Sources Bibliography

The following articles have been selected to supplement the diverse views presented in this chapter.

Kym Anderson and Bjørn Lomborg	"Free Trade, Free Labor, Free Growth," Project Syndicate, March 11, 2008. www.project-syndicate.org.
Doug Bandow	"A Free Trade Agreement with South Korea Would Promote Both Prosperity and Security," Cato Institute, October 20, 2010. www.cato.org.
Vern Buchanan	"Free Trade Means Jobs," *The Hill's Congress Blog*, August 29, 2011. http://thehill.com.
Eric Edmonds and Nina Pavcnik	"Trade and Child Labour," Vox, July 19, 2007. www.voxeu.org.
Daniel T. Griswold	"Seven Moral Arguments for Free Trade," *Cato Policy Report*, July/August 2001.
Nigel Hunt	"Modern Farming 'Harms Poor and Environment,'" *ABC Science*, April 16, 2008. www.abc.net.au.
Marc Lacey	"Bush Promotes Free Trade in Country with Widespread Child Labor," *New York Times*, March 12, 2007.
Tom Philpott	"Bloody Valentine: Child Slavery in Ivory Coast's Cocoa Fields," *Mother Jones*, February 14, 2012.
Shefali Sharma	"Free Trade and Human Rights: A Voyage into India's Countryside," *Think Forward*, April 14, 2011. http://iatp.typepad.com.
Witness for Peace	"Policy Analysis: Free Trade and Labor Rights," April 2, 2008. http://witnessforpeace.org.

OPPOSING
VIEWPOINTS®
SERIES

CHAPTER 4

What Are Some Issues Surrounding Free Trade and the Global Marketplace?

Chapter Preface

In a report on US trade and investment policy published in September 2011, a Council on Foreign Relations (CFR)–sponsored independent task force stated that one of the most effective ways to create jobs and to reverse the economic decline of the past decade was for the United States to "become a thriving trading nation."

The task force suggested that, through free trade, more Americans would be able to enjoy the benefits of global engagement, "within the framework of a strengthened, rules-based trading system." It is the belief of the task force that new trade and investment strategies will strengthen the US economy and open new horizons for all those who seek to participate in the global marketplace. It is imperative for the United States to take steps to changing and improving its record on free trade, stated the task force, because while the United States hesitates to implement new strategies, the rest of the world is not standing still but is forging ahead with new agreements and new marketing channel development.

In late 2011, the United States signed an agreement with South Korea, and on March 15, 2012, the Republic of Korea–United States free trade agreement (KORUS FTA) was entered into force. On the day of implementation, according to Export.gov, "almost 80 percent of U.S. industrial exports to Korea [became] duty-free, including aerospace equipment, agricultural equipment, auto parts, building products, chemicals, consumer goods, electrical equipment, environmental goods, travel goods, paper products, scientific equipment, and shipping and transportation equipment." Other purported benefits of KORUS include: nearly two-thirds of US agricultural products will be duty-free, stronger protection and enforcement of intellectual property rights in South Korea, and increased access to South Korea's $580 billion services market for highly competitive American companies.

In the lead-up to its signing, KORUS was vociferously opposed—with critics citing fears that the agreement would only benefit the US auto market, among other concerns. But there was also strong support for the free trade agreement, seen as a long overdue step toward economic recovery in the United States. One of the supporters was Ambassador Demetrios Marantis, chief international trade counsel for the Senate Committee on Finance, who spoke at the hearings on the US-South Korea free trade agreement on May 26, 2011.

"We are here at a critical moment in our nation's history, presented with a unique opportunity," Ambassador Marantis said. "Our economy is recovering, and for seven straight quarters, American exports have been a significant contributor to our economic growth. In 2010, nominal exports of goods and services were up 17 percent. This export growth already has supported hundreds of thousands of additional American jobs."

South Korea has far higher tariffs than does the United States and as a result of the free trade agreement, will see bigger changes in the variety and cost of goods after the trade deal takes effect. US growth could continue in parallel with South Korea's growth, argued supporters of KORUS, which would produce a win-win situation for both nations. "Within our grasp is the chance to put our recovery on solid footing and secure additional exports, growth, and jobs for Americans across this country. The U.S.-South Korea trade agreement will strengthen our trade and investment ties to South Korea's $1 trillion economy. It will bind a key strategic ally closer to us, anchor our economy to the dynamic Asia-Pacific, and help us keep our edge over international competition. It is a key element in our economic strategy in the region. Most importantly, the U.S.-South Korea trade agreement will create substantial export opportunities, establish strong enforcement provisions, and support new export-related jobs," Ambassador Marantis explained.

KORUS not only benefits those engaged in the auto and beef industries in the United States, proponents assert, but also benefits diverse group of other industries, many of which are never on the radar during pro and con discussions of such trade agreements. Among those who are purported to benefit from the free trade agreement are Florida growers, who enjoy an elimination of a tariff on frozen orange juice and a phase-out of the tariff on grapefruit; New Jersey, Maine, and Massachusetts blueberry and cranberry growers, who benefit from reductions in tariffs; and Delaware, Maryland, and West Virginia poultry and egg producers, who also benefit from a phaseout of tariffs.

The merits of global trade for US markets are explored in the following chapter of *Opposing Viewpoints: Free Trade*. Also examined are other issues relating to free trade in the modern global marketplace, including the best policies to support recovery from the global economic recession and guard against future global economic collapse; the effect of trade imbalances in a global marketplace; and the role of the United States in both global economic recovery and in raising living standards for workers worldwide.

> "Free trade has gone as far as it should go. The world's supranational organizations ... should draw up rules that allow countries—without jeopardising their trading opportunities—to reintroduce limited tariffs and opt out of regulations if they can show sufficient democratic support domestically for doing so."

Protective Trade Policies Are Needed to Prevent Global Economic Collapse

Peter Wilby

Peter Wilby has contributed articles on education to various newspapers and has served as editor of the Sunday Independent *and the* New Statesman. *In the following viewpoint, Wilby asserts that Europe and other parts of the world are experiencing a crisis of democracy, especially in terms of economics, as they are increasingly disenfranchised by restrictions on their liberty imposed by trade agreements. Wilby argues that in many cases, the expenses incurred by governments because of trade agreements result in reductions in spending on social programs and invest-*

ment in domestic industry. Further, Wilby asserts, economically powerful countries can persuade other countries to relax or even abandon environmental standards as part of a free trade agreement. All of this, Wilby concludes, has resulted in dire economic conditions in Europe. The solution, he contends, is to return to trade policies that place a premium on political sovereignty, social justice, and environmental issues, rather than on purely economic concerns.

As you read, consider the following questions:

1. According to Wilby, what is the ideal of the "Tory Eurosceptics"?

2. What does Wilby say the United States successfully challenged under NAFTA?

3. According to the viewpoint, what must governments and trade regulators agree to abandon?

The unravelling of the euro is not just an economic and financial crisis, it is also a crisis of democracy. The peoples of Europe are losing the capacity to determine their own futures. From Antwerp [Belgium] to Athens [Greece], they are being told that there is no alternative.

The people of Greece, Italy, Spain, Portugal and Ireland have already learned that they must accept programmes of austerity, reductions in employment protection and the sale of public assets to the private sector. If they haven't elected leaders willing to do what is necessary, unelected leaders will be imposed instead. The French and the Belgians know that they also must watch their step.

If you want to understand why stock markets seem resolved not to panic about a crisis that many politicians and economists predict will lead to armageddon—the FTSE [stock exchange owned jointly by the *Financial Times* and the London Stock Exchange] is less than 20% down on its 2007 peak, against nearly 50% down during the crisis that followed the collapse of Lehman Brothers—look no further. Capitalist investors see a Europe that is divesting itself of the democratic accountability that is so often a drag on the uninhibited pursuit of profit.

Does this mean that the Tory Eurosceptics were right all along? It does not. Their ideal is a Europe of free trade and zero government. Countries would compete by continually lowering taxes, cutting public services, driving down wages, weakening environmental protection, abolishing safety regulations, defanging trade unions, and so on. In their view, it is possible for a free trade area to flourish without the infringements of sovereignty that have become the hallmark of Brussels.

Free Trade Leads to Less Sovereignty

What they do not understand (or want to understand) is that, even without the ambition of political union that was behind the European project from its earliest days, free trade agreements always involve a progressive loss of sovereignty. Such agreements cannot long survive if one or more of the participating countries feels that others are taking an unfair advantage, by paying government subsidies to particular industries or by adopting regulations that, in effect, discriminate against foreign goods.

That is why every organisation designed to promote free trade—including the World Trade Organization [WTO] and the North American free trade area as well as the European Union [EU]—creates a gigantic bureaucracy to draw up rules, police their observance and resolve disputes. Free trade is driven by the desire to reduce the costs of transactions between economic players in different nations. The greater the diversity of regulation, the greater the transaction costs. The point of the euro was to cut the biggest transaction cost of all—changing money from one currency to another.

The left has more cause than the right to feel aggrieved by loss of sovereignty. The EU is actually the most democratic of free trade regimes; at least we elect MEPs [members of European Parliament] who have a modicum of power. But we don't elect anybody to the WTO. The EU often levels up regulation, requiring some countries to adopt, for example, higher minimums of environmental and consumer protection than they might otherwise do. More often, free trade levels down regulation and reduces the scope for taxation of corporations and capital.

Free Trade Undermines Domestic Choice

The global growth of inequality within nations is a direct result of free trade, which allows corporations to relocate with ease, capital to move across boundaries in search of lower costs, and companies to outsource labour to where production is cheapest. Profits have soared while wages have been depressed.

Free trade agreements undermine domestic attempts to impose environmental, health or safety standards. Under the NAFTA [North American Free Trade Agreement] treaty, US-owned companies successfully challenged restrictions by Mexican and Canadian authorities on, for example, the disposal of toxic waste and the use of gasoline additives. Several free trade agreements allow foreign investors to sue for damages when new regulations adversely affect their profits. For example, mining companies sued the South African government when they were required to alter their employment practices under a black empowerment programme.

Free trade, in other words, involves international agreement on the most contested areas of modern politics: the role and size of the state, levels of taxation, employees' rights, the extent to which we should protect the environment, and so on. It is not just the EU that needs rethinking; it is the whole world trade regime. The present EU crisis is just an extreme

Limits Must Be Placed on Energy Exports to Protect American Interests

In 2011, the U.S. became a net exporter of petroleum products for the first time in 62 years—exporting more than two million barrels of gasoline, diesel and other products per day. Refined petroleum products actually became America's leading export in 2011, with more than $100 billion in refined product sent overseas according to the Commerce Department, at a time when Americans experienced near-record petroleum prices.

We are concerned about the inadequacy of the existing federal processes which govern the export of all of these American energy commodities. . . .

We believe that four key considerations should guide our determination of whether energy exports are in the national interest: national security; energy security; economic impacts, including impacts on domestic energy prices and America's manufacturing competiveness; and environmental protection. . . .

It would be unwise for our country to go down a road in which we incur the potential environmental impacts of increased energy development, while sending overseas the economic benefits of these greater supplies. . . .

Unlimited export of energy commodities could undermine the economic opportunity before us and result in unwanted economic and environmental impacts.

Ron Wyden and Edward J. Markey,
"Letter from Senator Ron Wyden and Representative
Edward J. Markey to President Barack H. Obama,
Concerning Energy Exports," May 31, 2012.
http://democrats.naturalresources.house.gov.

example of what happens if you put maximisation of economic activity ahead of all other considerations, such as social justice, democratic consent and local cultures.

If the single currency were dumped, the EU would still make rules and regulations to facilitate free trade. If the EU itself ceased to exist, the sovereignty of its members would still be inhibited by other trade agreements. Such agreements inevitably take decision making to a level beyond the control of national electorates. The EU is criticised for its "democratic deficit", but there are many worse examples among international trade bodies.

Restoring Sovereignty Will Lead to Increased Economic Stability and Solve Social and Environmental Problems

Is there an answer? Under the pressure of financial crisis, the danger is that the world reverts in a disorderly manner to the 1930s, when countries rushed to raise tariffs, impose import quotas and devalue their currencies. Amid the chaos, authoritarian right-wing regimes flourished. That will happen again—perhaps even in Athens, Rome, Lisbon or Madrid—unless governments and trade regulators can agree to abandon the dogma that free trade is, everywhere and always, an absolute good. They should recognise that democracy is a greater good and that it is, and always will be, located in nation-states.

Free trade has gone as far as it should go. The world's supranational organisations, including the WTO and the EU, should draw up rules that allow countries—without jeopardising their trading opportunities—to reintroduce limited tariffs and opt out of regulations if they can show sufficient democratic support domestically for doing so.

Above all, they should design rules to regulate global finance—including a financial transactions tax, which would be impossible for any single country under the present regime—and to permit nation-states to regulate cross-border financial transactions. The focus needs to switch from maximising trade to maximising democratic accountability, economic stability, social justice and the survival of the planet. It may sound impossible but so, in the 1940s, did global free trade. All world leaders need to do is to change their focus, and soon.

"*The best insurance against protectionism . . . is macroeconomic stimulus. Boosting demand at home will reduce the temptation to divert it from abroad.*"

Stimulating Market Demand Is the Best Way to Ensure Recovery from Global Financial Crisis

The Economist

The Economist *is a weekly newspaper focused on international politics and business news and opinion. In the following viewpoint, the* Economist *discusses the growing risk of protectionism in light of the global economy facing its worst recession in decades, positing that protectionism would further disrupt the already ailing economy. While it might seem to make sense to countries to protect their own interests in a time of crisis, the* Economist *explains, history has shown that tariffs and other protectionist policies can worsen economic conditions for everyone, as did the Smoot-Hawley Tariff Act during the Great Depression. Although economic partnerships and trade agreements are essential, the* Economist *concludes, the best way to hasten recovery of the global marketplace is to take measures to boost domestic spending.*

As you read, consider the following questions:

1. According to the viewpoint, a cut in the target for what rate shows how fearful America's policy makers are?

2. Prior to 2009, when was the last time that global trade volumes shrank, according to the viewpoint?

3. What does the *Economist* say could be prompted by movements in currency exchange rates?

This Christmas [2008] the world economy offers few reasons for good cheer. As credit contracts and asset prices plunge, demand across the globe is shrivelling. Rich countries collectively face the severest recession since the Second World War: This week's cut in the target for the federal funds rate to between zero and 0.25% shows how fearful America's policy makers are. And conditions are deteriorating fast too in emerging economies, which have been whacked by tumbling exports and the drying up of foreign finance.

This news is bad enough in itself; but it also poses the biggest threat to open markets in the modern era of globalisation. For the first time in more than a generation, two of the engines of global integration—trade and capital flows—are simultaneously shifting into reverse. The World Bank says that net private capital flows to emerging economies in 2009 are likely to be only half the record $1 trillion of 2007, while global trade volumes will shrink for the first time since 1982.

Protectionist Policies Appear Promising but Would Make Matters Worse

This twin shift will force wrenching adjustments. Countries that have relied on exports to drive growth, from China to Germany, will slump unless they can boost domestic demand quickly. The flight of private capital means emerging economies with current-account deficits face a drought of financing as well as export earnings. There is a risk that in their discomfort, governments turn to an old, but false, friend: protectionism. Integration has less appeal when pain rather than prosperity is ricocheting across borders. It will be tempting to prop up domestic jobs and incomes by diverting demand from abroad with export subsidies, tariffs and cheaper currencies.

The lessons of history, though, are clear. The economic isolationism of the 1930s, epitomised by America's Smoot-Hawley Tariff [Act], cruelly intensified the [Great] Depression. To be sure, the World Trade Organization (WTO) and its multilateral trading rules are a bulwark against protection on that scale. But today's globalised economy, with far-flung supply chains and just-in-time delivery, could be disrupted by policies much less dramatic than the Smoot-Hawley act. A modest shift away from openness—well within the WTO's rules—would be enough to turn the recession of 2009 much nastier. Incremental protection of that sort is, alas, all too plausible.

Fair-Weather Free Traders Are Increasing in Number

In many countries, politicians' fealty to open markets is already more rhetorical than real. In November the leaders of the G20 group of big rich and emerging economies promised to eschew any new trade barriers for a year and to work hard for agreement on the Doha Round of trade talks by the end of December. Within days, two of the G20 countries, Russia and India, raised tariffs on cars and steel, respectively. And the year is ending with no Doha breakthrough in sight.

As economies weaken, popular scepticism of open markets will surely grow. Among rich countries, that danger is greatest in America, where grumbles were heard long before recession

set in. The new Congress, with bigger Democratic majorities, has a decidedly less trade-friendly hue. Barack Obama's campaign rhetoric left an impression of a man in two minds about trade, which he has since done nothing to dispel.

Now that their exports are faltering, emerging economies too may become less keen on trade. The WTO's rules allow them plenty of scope: After two decades of unilateral tariff-cutting most, of their tariffs are well below their "bound" rates, the ceilings agreed in the trade club. On average they could triple their import levies without breaking the rules.

Handouts Are Not Being Evenly or Wisely Distributed

Politicians from Washington to Beijing are being pressed to help troubled industries, regardless of the consequences for trade. A bailout of Detroit's carmakers, whatever its final extent, will be a discriminatory subsidy. As China's exporters go bust by the thousand, industries from textiles to steel have been promised handouts and rebates. Subsidies will beget more subsidies: Nicolas Sarkozy, France's president, says that Europe will turn into an "industrial wasteland" if it too does not prop up its manufacturers. They will also invite retaliation. With China's bilateral trade surplus at a record high even as America's economy slumps, Congress will not take kindly to Beijing's bolstering of its exporters.

Exchange-rate movements could also prompt protectionist responses. Chinese officials have said publicly that they will not push down the yuan, and their currency has risen in trade-weighted terms. However, it did slip against the dollar in late November. Viewed from America, China still seems to be following a cheap-yuan policy. A Sino-American trade spat is all too plausible.

Add all this together and it is hard for a free trader not to worry. So what is to be done? The first requirement is political leadership, especially from America and China. At a minimum, both must avoid beggar-thy-neighbour policies. Second, a conclusion of the Doha Round would help. A deal would reduce the risk of broader backsliding by cutting many countries' bound tariffs—and it would establish Mr Obama's multilateral credentials. Third—Doha deal or not—is greater transparency. A good recent idea is that the WTO publicise any new barriers, whether or not they are allowed by its rules.

The best insurance against protectionism, however, is macroeconomic stimulus. Boosting demand at home will reduce the temptation to divert it from abroad. By historical standards, policy makers are acting aggressively, as the Federal Reserve did this week. But the effort is unevenly, and poorly, distributed. Emerging economies from which capital is fleeing have little room to boost spending. Some creditor countries (notably Germany) are holding back on fiscal stimulus, while the world's biggest borrower (America) is acting the most boldly. A bigger push to boost domestic demand in creditor countries coupled with more help, through the IMF [International Monetary Fund], to cushion cash-strapped emerging economies would ease the world economy's adjustment and brighten the prospects for free trade. In the 1930s protectionism flourished largely because of macroeconomic failures. That must not happen this time.

> "The [Trans-Pacific Partnership] agreement has the potential to become a new paradigm for trade agreements, to help the United States reassert its position in the Asia-Pacific, and to begin the process of defragmenting international trade."

Flexible Trade Partnerships Attract More Global Stakeholders and Offer Greater Investment Return

Meredith Kolsky Lewis

Meredith Kolsky Lewis is senior lecturer and codirector of the New Zealand Centre of International Economic Law at the Victoria University of Wellington. In the following viewpoint, Lewis discusses the US involvement in the Trans-Pacific Partnership (TPP), which, she asserts, has the potential to expand into a free trade agreement with countries of the Asia-Pacific region. A free trade agreement with the Asia-Pacific would provide, Lewis contends, the United States with greater leverage in the region but would also greatly increase the potential for more countries to

Meredith Kolsky Lewis, "The Trans-Pacific Partnership: New Paradigm or Wolf in Sheep's Clothing?," *Boston College International and Comparative Law Review*, vol. 34, no. 1, 2011, pp. 38–44, 51–52. Copyright © 2011 by Boston College International and Comparative Law Review. All rights reserved. Reproduced by permission.

participate in multilateral free trade. Details regarding particular regulations represent obstacles to US involvement in the TPP, but President Barack Obama, is, Lewis concludes, wise to pursue such involvement, because an eventual free trade agreement with the Asia-Pacific would provide opportunities to increase US market involvement and economic returns on its investments.

As you read, consider the following questions:

1. What did Secretary of State James Baker caution would be a mistake, according to the viewpoint?

2. What changes requested by the United States would New Zealand likely oppose, according to Lewis?

3. According to Lewis, how must the United States avoid "shooting itself in the foot" in negotiating the TPP?

Twenty years ago [in 1989], the then secretary of state James Baker famously cautioned that it would be a mistake for the United States to permit "a line to be drawn down the middle of the Pacific" with the United States on one side, separated from Asian countries on the other. Notwithstanding this warning, we have seen numerous models for economic integration in East Asia and the Asia-Pacific that exclude the United States from their formulations. ASEAN [Association of Southeast Asian Nations] Plus 3, ASEAN Plus 6, and an East Asian FTA [free trade agreement] comprising Japan, Korea, and China, are all different visions for deeper regional economic integration, and each has deliberately omitted the United States from the equation. If the United States could succeed in negotiating the TPP [Trans-Pacific Partnership]— and additionally succeed in selling the TPP as the basis for broader expansion within APEC [Asia-Pacific Economic Cooperation]—it could represent a major step toward achieving President [Barack] Obama's goal of engaging with Asia, and would erase the line down the middle of the Pacific, which China, Japan, and perhaps others, might prefer to draw.

An expanded TPP could lead to a different path toward Asian economic integration, which would have neither ASEAN nor the three major East Asian economies as its driver, and which would instead have the United States as a central participant.

If the expanded TPP becomes the basis for a Free Trade Area of the Asia-Pacific (FTAAP), Asian integration will likely develop along lines more similar to those envisioned (even if primarily in an aspirational sense) by the members of the Asia-Pacific Economic Cooperation (APEC) than those being contemplated in the context of ASEAN Plus arrangements or an East Asian FTA. In particular, an expanded TPP would lead to a trans-Pacific integration rather than an intra-Asian integration.

The Trans-Pacific Partnership Has Great Potential to Expand Multilateral Free Trade

The United States' decision to negotiate to join the TPP is therefore quite savvy. By joining the TPP, the United States has the potential not only to thwart efforts to shape Asian economic regionalism models that exclude it, but, if the TPP expansion is successful and continues, the United States will also be a leader and agenda setter with respect to the parameters of a future FTAAP. Further, if the TPP grows into an FTAAP, the global economic order would also be altered. At present, there are three major economic blocs—the Americas, Europe, and Asia—and the American bloc is not necessarily the most economically powerful among these. An Asia-Pacific integration has the potential to alter the balance into a two-bloc model comprising Europe and the Asia-Pacific, with the latter including Asia, the United States, Oceania, and much of South America. Therefore, joining the TPP could help the United States play an active role in altering the regional power balance, thereby inserting itself into what is likely to be the more powerful of two large blocs as opposed to remaining on the wrong side of a divided Pacific.

Depending on how the expansion is structured, the TPP additionally has the potential to multilateralize some aspects of regionalism, which would help facilitate the creation of an FTAAP. In other words, the famous "spaghetti bowl" of overlapping and inconsistent FTAs proliferating the globe could be partially untangled if a large group of countries could agree to a harmonized set of commitments to which other countries could accede. The TPP—and ultimately an FTAAP—has the potential to serve as a model of open regionalism and a stepping stone toward multilateral trade liberalization, rather than the stumbling block that FTAs more commonly present.

The Trans-Pacific Partnership Represents a Significant Expansion of Free Trade Agreements

By combining a high-standards, comprehensive trade agreement with an open accession provision and the United States as a party, the TPP has the potential to create a new paradigm for trade agreements. Rather than presenting the usual two-country model in which both countries pick and choose the areas they wish to liberalize, the TPP would draw together multiple countries from both sides of the Pacific. The TPP has the potential to be far more comprehensive than the average FTA. With the United States as a party, other countries will be interested in joining the TPP, and doing so would require significant liberalization commitments. If the TPP were negotiated on these terms, it is possible—perhaps even likely—that the TPP would lead to an FTAAP.

The Trans-Pacific Partnership Has Implications for the WTO

If the TPP does expand in the near future into a larger agreement that captures a significant percentage of trans-Pacific trade, it may impact the ability of WTO [World Trade Organization] members to complete the current [2011] Doha Round of negotiations. The nature of this impact could be negative because the United States and other TPP members could determine that expanding the TPP is an easier and more fruitful path towards new trade liberalization gains than is the multilateral framework. On the other hand, the growth of the TPP could have a positive impact on the Doha Round. USTR [United States Trade Representative] Ron Kirk has indicated that he believes the TPP will complement the WTO negotiations. Although Kirk did not explain his comment, it seems feasible that he is correct. Countries that are not currently a part of the TPP discussions may fear that the world is splitting into large trading blocs from which they are currently excluded, and thus be incentivized to reinvigorate the Doha Round. In particular, India and Brazil may determine it is worth giving additional WTO concessions to refocus the United States on the WTO.

There Are Potential Pitfalls for the TPP

Although the USTR appears to be enthusiastically pursuing the TPP, and the other countries involved in the agreement seem to be similarly motivated, TPP expansion is far from guaranteed. There are a number of issues that must be resolved before an expanded TPP can become a reality. These issues comprise substantive obstacles in the negotiating process as well as procedural hurdles that must be addressed once an agreement is reached. Moreover, these issues will significantly affect whether the TPP will multilateralize trade among APEC members, ultimately leading to an FTAAP. . . .

Substantive Negotiating Challenges

In most FTA negotiations, there are a number of issues relating to substantive coverage that pose challenges to resolve. Although each partner stands to benefit from the market access liberalization measures taken by the trading partner, each partner in turn faces domestic opposition to liberalizing its

The United States in the Trans-Pacific Partnership

On November 12, 2011, the leaders of the nine Trans-Pacific Partnership countries—Australia, Brunei, Chile, Malaysia, New Zealand, Peru, Singapore, Vietnam, and the United States—announced the achievement of the broad outlines of an ambitious, 21st-century Trans-Pacific Partnership (TPP) agreement that will enhance trade and investment among the TPP partner countries, promote innovation, economic growth and development, and support the creation and retention of jobs. . . .

The agreement will include:

• Core issues traditionally included in trade agreements, including industrial goods, agriculture, and textiles as well as rules on intellectual property, technical barriers to trade, labor, and environment.

• Cross-cutting issues not previously in trade agreements, such as making the regulatory systems of TPP countries more compatible so U.S. companies can operate more seamlessly in TPP markets, and helping innovative, job-creating, small- and medium-sized enterprises participate more actively in international trade.

• New emerging trade issues such as addressing trade and investment in innovative products and services, including digital technologies, and ensuring state-owned enterprises compete fairly with private companies and do not distort competition in ways that put U.S. companies and workers at a disadvantage.

"The United States in the Trans-Pacific Partnership,"
Office of the United States Trade Representative,
November 2011. http://ustr.gov.

home market for goods and services produced or supplied domestically. The P4 Agreement [original Trans-Pacific Strategic Economic Partnership Agreement between Brunei, Chile, New Zealand, and Singapore] was relatively unique in being able to overcome some of these obstacles and achieve a highly comprehensive agreement, at least with respect to trade in goods. With the addition of the United States, however, the TPP negotiations are more typical of many bilateral FTA negotiations. Accordingly, there are a number of potential issues regarding substantive matters within the negotiation. This section briefly discusses two of these issues: agriculture and intellectual property.

1. Agriculture

The United States has historically refused to liberalize most aspects of trade in agriculture in its FTAs, yet the P4 countries have agreed to comprehensive removal of tariffs on agricultural products. How much of its agricultural sector the United States will be willing to include in its TPP commitments, is likely to be a significant issue. Roughly half of New Zealand's exports to the United States are agricultural products that the United States considers sensitive: primarily dairy, lamb, and beef. The U.S. dairy industry has already reacted with alarm to the idea of an agreement that could involve New Zealand dairy products gaining improved access to the U.S. market, and thirty senators signed a letter to USTR Ron Kirk expressing concern in this regard.

For New Zealand, excluding dairy from the agreement would be a very hard sell. Nevertheless, New Zealand has very little to offer the United States in exchange for including dairy. In fact, the United States may have little to gain from forming an alliance with New Zealand. The New Zealand market is already highly liberalized, so there would be only minimal gains in the form of improved market access. And New Zealand is a small market, currently accounting for less than .05% of U.S. exports. Thus, notwithstanding New

Zealand's long-term goal of achieving an FTA with the United States, it may be that New Zealand does not have enough to offer the United States, or (admittedly less likely) that the United States' demands will result in insufficient payoffs for New Zealand.

2. Intellectual Property

A second issue that may prove challenging in the negotiations is intellectual property protection. The United States generally includes provisions in its FTAs that are referred to as "TRIPS-plus" in that they provide higher levels of protection than is required by the WTO's Trade-Related Aspects of Intellectual Property Rights (TRIPS) agreement. This does not pose an issue for countries that already have FTAs—including TRIPS-plus provisions—with the United States—such as Australia. Nevertheless, there are aspects of the Australia–United States Free Trade Agreement (AUSFTA) that are inconsistent with the United States–Singapore FTA with respect to intellectual property protection. For example, the United States–Singapore agreement does not prohibit the practice of parallel importation [importation of a patented or trademarked product from a country in which it is already marketed], whereas the AUSFTA does prohibit parallel importation.

For a small market economy such as New Zealand, permitting parallel imports makes good economic sense; indeed, New Zealand allows parallel imports in its domestic law and has yet to agree to limit such imports in any of its FTAs. Presumably the United States will want the TPP to include provisions restricting parallel imports, which will be opposed at a minimum by New Zealand and Singapore. The AUSFTA also imposes restrictions that affect how Australia purchases prescription drugs for its public health system. It is likely that the United States would want New Zealand to make similar changes, which New Zealand would oppose. . . .

The United States Could Greatly Benefit from Joining the Trans-Pacific Partnership

The Obama administration is wise to negotiate for a Trans-Pacific Partnership. Such an agreement has the potential to reassert the United States' position as a leader and economic participant on both sides of the Pacific. It also represents the best chance, among the options otherwise in play, for the United States to play a role in shaping a future Free Trade Area of the Asia-Pacific (FTAAP). The TPP agreement has the potential to act as a building block toward further liberalization, and to multilateralize some of the fragmentation resulting from the panoply of FTAs today.

If a TPP agreement is reached in the form of one unified agreement with common market access schedules, it will have a greater potential to attract more participants and meaningfully reduce trade barriers among a growing circle of nations. Nevertheless, there is a significant risk that the TPP will not live up to its potential. The more the TPP looks like a series of bilateral U.S. FTAs with exclusions for products the United States considers sensitive, the less likely the TPP will attract other countries to accede. Thus, the United States must carefully assess its goals for the TPP. Moreover, the United States must be careful not to shoot itself in the foot by following a "business as usual" approach, if it truly intends to create a high-standards agreement that will be a model for an FTAAP. The traditional U.S. FTA model is not as likely as the model advocated by Australia, New Zealand, and Singapore, to achieve the result the USTR claims to be pursuing. Nonetheless, it will be surprising if the United States agrees to diverge from its previous negotiating strategies and assent to the model advocated by Australia, New Zealand, and Singapore.

There are a number of impediments that may torpedo the TPP agreement before it is concluded, and other factors that could render any agreement of no more significance than any other U.S. FTA. Nevertheless, the TPP agreement has the *po-*

tential to become a new paradigm for trade agreements, to help the United States reassert its position in the Asia-Pacific, and to begin the process of defragmenting international trade. The potential payoffs are significant and important: Hopefully the United States can resist the temptation to pursue "business as usual"—an approach that would actually undermine its strategic objectives—and instead take the necessary steps to achieve those goals.

"*We have reached the end point of glo-*
balization as we have known it. It can-
not continue as before, because the
United States is essentially tapped out.
Goliath has fallen and cannot get up."

The US Economy Must Recover for the Global Marketplace to Succeed

William Greider

William Greider, a prominent political journalist and author,
has been a reporter for more than thirty-five years. He is the au-
thor of the national best sellers One World, Ready or Not; Se-
crets of the Temple; *and* Who Will Tell the People? *In the fol-*
lowing viewpoint, Greider outlines the grim economic situation
that has resulted from the United States' reduced purchasing
power following the global economic crisis. Although China has
not, according to Greider, engaged in market activities—includ-
ing currency manipulation—its actions have had a massive im-
pact on the world economy simply due to the sheer size of its
population. Furthermore, Greider explains, China has failed to
recognize that without the United States to purchase its exports
and the exports of other countries, the global economy will col-

*lapse. In order to ensure its own economic stability, and, conse-
quently, the stability of the global marketplace, Greider concludes, the United States must impose restrictions and regulations
on marketplace activity that are beneficial to Americans and to
the US economy.*

As you read, consider the following questions:

1. How long was the complaint filed by United Steelworkers, according to the viewpoint?

2. According to Greider, why are expanding trade deficits
   viewed as the most ominous development for Americans?

3. How can public subsidies be used to ensure that companies act in the best interests of the United States, according to Greider?

The world economy is on the brink again, facing a crisis of
epic dimensions for reasons largely obscured by the in-
flamed politics of 2010. Against their wishes, the United States
and China have been drawn into an increasingly nasty and
dangerous fight over currencies and trade. American politicians, especially desperate Democrats, have framed the conflict
in familiar moral terms—a melodrama of America wronged—
and demand retaliation. Other nations, sensing the risk of a
larger breakdown, have begun to take protective measures. Every man for himself. The center is not holding.

The political fray obscures the fact that the basic economic
problem is larger than any single nation and stalks the global
trading system itself. There is a huge hole in the world—a
massive loss of demand. Think of the trade wars as the largest
producers fighting over an abrupt shortage of buyers. Financial collapse and recession, with falling income, defaulting
debt and rising unemployment, made the hole. In other times,
Washington would have stepped in to impose policy solutions
and create market demand as the global system's buyer of last

resort. This time, Goliath is gravely weakened, both in economic strength and political authority.

The political push-pull zeroes in on China. Beijing is accused of playing dirty, stealing jobs, production and wealth. Washington imposes a penalty tariff on Chinese tires and tubular steel. Beijing pushes back with a tariff on US poultry. President [Barack] Obama once again urges China to stop manipulating its currency to underprice Chinese exports and stymie US goods going the other way. China once again blows off his request. United Steelworkers ups the ante by filing a 5,800-page complaint detailing how China is scheming to corner the global market in green technologies. Obama promptly orders an investigation. "What do the Americans want?" asks the vice chair of Beijing's National Development and Reform Commission. "Do they want fair trade? Or an earnest dialogue?. . . I don't think they want any of this. I think more likely, the Americans just want votes." He has a point. But so do American politicians, who think China's hardball industrial strategy has had something to do with America's anemic recovery. The House, divided on everything else, voted 348–79 in September [2010] to authorize tariffs on nearly all Chinese imports if Beijing does not relent in its currency game.

China's Market Actions Are Unpopular with Americans and Others

The US public seems to agree with the harsh stance. A *Wall Street Journal* poll found that 53 percent (including 61 percent of Tea Party adherents) think free trade globalization has hurt the US economy. Only 17 percent think it has helped. But the trouble with Americans claiming injured innocence is that it blinds them to the complexities of the predicament. The fact is, the United States and China, motivated by different but mutually reinforcing reasons, collaborated to create the unbalanced trading system. American multinationals eagerly sought access to China's market. The Chinese wanted factories and the modern technologies needed to develop a first-class industrial base. American companies agreed to the basic trade-off: China would let them in to make and sell stuff, and they would share technology and teach Chinese partners how it's done. Not coincidentally, US corporations also gained enormous bargaining power over workers back home by threatening to go abroad for cheaper labor if unions didn't give wage concessions.

Washington blessed the deal. Both parties were convinced decades ago that improving the fortunes of globalizing banks and businesses was in the broad national interest. The [President Bill] Clinton administration capitulated to Chinese negotiators in 2000, admitting China to the World Trade Organization while giving up legal tools that could have controlled China's appetites.

Chinese officials understand, even if many Americans do not, that they are essentially doing what the trading system has allowed or at least tolerated from many others. Washington grumbled when Japan and then South Korea, Taiwan and Singapore pursued similar development strategies. Arrogant US policy makers assumed that these rivals would eventually adopt the American model and become more like us. They never really have.

The problem is that when a nation of 1.3 billion successfully advances along this road, it blows out the lights. Decades ago, when Washington scolded Japanese officials for violating free trade orthodoxy, they bowed humbly and made agreeable noises. The Chinese don't bother. They are unabashed because they have always been much more up front about their intentions. In the early 1990s, Beijing published a series of directives for major industrial sectors, describing precisely how the state intended to direct the rise of its industrial base. China manipulates its currency—though so do other governments when it serves their interests (indignant senators bash China for depressing its currency, but Washington is doing the very same thing to the dollar through the money spigots of the Federal Reserve). The Chinese also know that Japan suffered years of depressed growth after Washington pushed it into raising the value of its currency. China pirates US intellectual property, and it suppresses wages to attract factories from the United States and elsewhere. It lures major US multinationals by offering tax breaks and subsidies—but it also compels the companies to share their precious technologies with Chinese partners, who are always majority owners.

China's Rapid Expansion Weakens the United States

Which brings us to the present crisis. China's exports exploded toward the end of the Clinton years and expanded even more ferociously under George W. Bush. So did the off-loading of US jobs and manufacturing. China's wave of new competition crashed over every industrial economy, but disruptions were most devastating for the United States. American trade deficits soared, peaking at close to 6 percent of GDP [gross domestic product] in 2006. Imports from China dwarfed exports in sector after sector, including many advanced technological goods developed in America. The goods are often made by US companies, but not here. The US economy has been buying more than it produces—a lot more—and borrowing from foreign creditors, most heavily from China, to do so.

"I admire the Chinese for recognizing the world economy is still a jungle, despite all of its legal trappings," says Alan Tonelson, a conservative trade critic at the US Business and Industry Council. "But here's the problem. They don't seem to understand that unless the US economy recovers its financial and economic health, the entire world will come crashing down. The reason is, we won't be able to serve any longer as the impart sponge that buys from everyone else."

We have reached the end point of globalization as we have known it. It cannot continue as before, because the United States is essentially tapped out. Goliath has fallen and cannot get up. Who will lend a hand? Not China, obviously, but also not Japan and the Asian Tigers, or the European nations. All are dealing with their own problems. All but the smallest economies run perennial trade surpluses with the United States. Giving up some of those surpluses means surrendering some portion of domestic growth in order to stabilize the system. No one wants to go first. This is a dangerous impasse, the kind that can easily slip into a general unwinding—that is, depression—if not resolved smartly. "The world is no longer in a common foxhole . . . but in many different foxholes," observes economist Paul McCulley of PIMCO [Pacific Investment Management Company], the world's largest bond house. Japan and South Korea devalue their currencies to protect their exports (so has the United States). Brazil puts limits on capital inflows to stop foreign money from destabilizing its economy. Currency war is a surrogate for trade war, one of the few levers governments can still manipulate unilaterally.

For Americans the most ominous development is that trade deficits, after shrinking during the recession, are expanding rapidly again. That stands in the way of recovery and helps explain why the federal stimulus of 2009 had less punch than expected. The trap is illustrated by a few recent statistics: The US economy expanded in the second quarter of 2010 by an anemic annualized rate of 1.7 percent. During those same months, however, the nation's trade deficit expanded by 3.5 percent. Do the arithmetic: The US economy would have grown at a much healthier rate if it weren't for its dependence on products made elsewhere. Yet getting different results will take much more than currency adjustments. It means reforming the dynamics of global trade and the US industrial structure, not just the bad habits of American consumers.

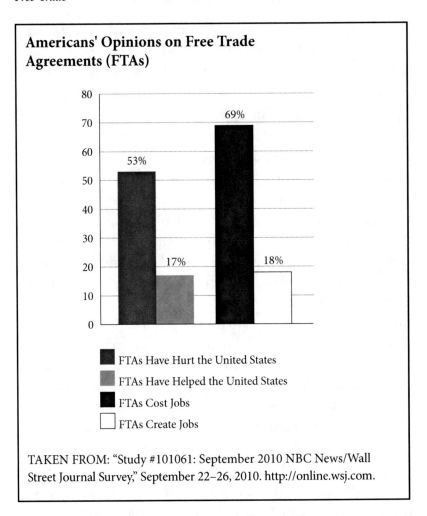

Americans' Opinions on Free Trade Agreements (FTAs)

- ■ FTAs Have Hurt the United States
- ▨ FTAs Have Helped the United States
- ■ FTAs Cost Jobs
- □ FTAs Create Jobs

TAKEN FROM: "Study #101061: September 2010 NBC News/Wall Street Journal Survey," September 22–26, 2010. http://online.wsj.com.

President Obama Must Act Unilaterally to Set Limits

President Obama, unlike his predecessors, understands the problem. He has been trying for the past year to persuade foreign governments to cooperate, with meager results so far. Obama told G20 leaders [a group of twenty finance ministers and central bank governors] in April 2009, "The world has become accustomed to the United States being a voracious consumer market and the engine that drives a lot of economic growth worldwide. . . . [But] if there's going to be renewed growth, it can't just be the United States as the engine. Everybody is going to have to pick up the pace." At the G20 meeting this past June, the president was more explicit. "After years of taking on too much debt," he said, "Americans cannot—and will not—borrow and buy the world's way to lasting prosperity. No nation should assume its path to prosperity is simply paved with exports to the United States."

There's no easy road to peace. The target is not only China but some of Washington's old friends, who run bloated surpluses at US expense. The Obama administration pushed concrete measures at the meeting of finance ministers in South Korea in October. Treasury Secretary Tim Geithner proposed a new global rule that would require nations running trade surpluses to shrink them to no more than 4 percent of GDP, presumably by buying more imports from debtor countries, while debtor nations like the United States would have to reduce deficits by the same amount, to less than 4 percent.

Geithner's strict numerical limits were not accepted, but his proposal represents an important first step—a US administration coming to terms with American weakness and stepping away from the free trade dogma that led to the crisis. The president recognizes the global nature of the problem. But I expect he will be compelled to take a tougher step—acting unilaterally. He will have to act for the United States in ways that get other nations, especially China, to take him seriously. Washington could, for example, declare a financial emergency, enacting legislation to put a ceiling on US trade deficits and begin a gradual process of reducing them. That would be a signal to exporting nations and multinational corporations that the good old days are over. But shrinking the trade deficits, important as it will be, is not sufficient. Washington must also change the rules for how American business and finance operate. Only in America do multinationals get to behave like free riders, with no strings attached. They harvest public money as subsidies and investment capital, they are protected by US armed forces and diplomacy, and they are rescued when they get into trouble. It is a one-way relationship, and the American public knows it.

US corporations and banks remain free to move jobs and production whenever and wherever corporate strategy dictates, regardless of the consequences for the economy. Government can stop this by forcing them to serve the broader national interest. This is not as radical as it may sound. Every other leading industrial nation does it, one way or another. They impose limits on corporate strategy, either in formally binding ways or through political and cultural pressure, to ensure that good jobs and the best value-added production remains at home.

Washington can accomplish this only through unilateral action, not free trade agreements. It has to rewrite trade law, tax law and policies on workforce development and subsidy. Resistance will be fierce, given the power and influence of big-name banks and corporations, but the public will surely support efforts to make the big guys serve the country's well-being.

If Washington doesn't make these broad structural changes, another popular idea will prove illusory—that US manufacturing can be rebuilt around green technologies. China is already doing this, and is far ahead. It has 35 percent of the global market in solar panels and is poised to dominate other green technologies. The United States, in fact, has swelling trade deficits in this sector. American companies work both sides of the competition, collecting subsidies on both ends.

Labor and Manufacturing Reforms Are Key

Doubters may say that Obama doesn't have the nerve to tackle this problem. They may be right. But the president is clearly thinking along these lines. He is the first president in thirty years to call for restoration of US manufacturing. This past summer he pushed modest tax measures that give a small advantage to home-based producers. The impact was so meager that Republicans didn't bother to object. But the GOP may also have grasped that measures favoring US factories over foreign ones will be wildly popular with voters. Obama repeated the message before a Labor Day audience in Milwaukee, saying, "I don't want to see solar panels and wind turbines and electric cars made in China. I want them made right here in the United States of America."

The best evidence for Obama's potential comes from liberal labor reformers fighting the trench warfare on trade cases while advocating for more fundamental reforms. "The president has been true to his word and very supportive on trade-law enforcement—better than any president since before NAFTA [North American Free Trade Agreement]," says Leo Gerard, president of the United Steelworkers. "The president is trying to do the right thing on outsourcing, on taking away tax breaks from multinationals."

Senator Sherrod Brown of Ohio cites a series of White House decisions on trade and stimulus spending that saved 400 jobs in Youngstown, more jobs in Lorain and 1,000 steel industry jobs overall. "On each case, we had to beat the hell out of the White House," Brown allows, "but this White House is more open to manufacturing than any in memory. When the president focuses on the facts, he comes down on our side." Brown and Gerard hope to build visibility and mobilize popular support that will push the president and Congress to embrace more ambitious reforms. "They have a manufacturing strategy, but it is not yet a manufacturing policy," Brown says. . . .

The US Government Must Implement Regulations on Companies to Ensure Economic Recovery and Stability

Multinationals drive the destructive cycle but are also its prisoners. They cannot quit on their own without losing out to other companies. Only governments, acting together and individually, have the power to reverse the cycle before it is too late. The US government can confront these negative forces by altering bottom-line incentives for multinationals based here. It can do this through the tax code, by levying a stiff penalty on corporations that continue to offshore more production than they create at home.

Public subsidies are another leverage point. Instead of competing with other nations to provide the biggest subsidies, Washington could disqualify companies from any form of subsidy unless they agree to accept concrete performance terms reflecting national loyalty. The obvious means of enforcement is a staple device of American capitalism—the enforceable contract. When GE [General Electric] gets capital and other financial support from taxpayers, it makes no promises about how long the jobs will stay at home or even if jobs will be created. The government should get it in writing: If the company is unwilling to make such commitments, it won't receive any money. If GE decides to break the promise, the contract will make the company return the money or surrender the security bond required up front. Government, in other words, should mimic practices that are routine on Wall Street and in corporate finance.

If Washington also adopts sterner measures to reduce its trade deficits, the discipline will alter strategic decision making by firms like GE. A collar that steadily closes the trade gap would create risks for offshoring companies and capital investment abroad, since foreign production would lose its assured access to the American consumer. A border tax on social costs would provide a similar way to defend American standards from free riders overseas. If, for example, the United States decides it must raise costs for domestic producers to reduce pollution or hydrocarbon consumption, foreign factories should be required to pay an equivalent border tax on imports if their country of origin does not impose similar costs on production. An emergency general tariff would be a more extreme version of the same principle.

All these suggestions are deeply disruptive to global commerce, and, yes, many would raise prices for Americans. But the country's predicament is a historic emergency that cannot wait for market solutions. The United States must, in effect, decide that its role as Goliath is over. It's time to act like a nation again rather than as the global overseer. If Barack Obama doesn't find the nerve to act, maybe the next president will.

> "If the world is to continue enjoying the benefits of global trade and finance, the global imbalances have to be unwound."

Trade Imbalances Must Be Corrected to Ensure Global Prosperity

Simon Tilford

Simon Tilford is chief economist at the Centre for European Reform in London. In the following viewpoint, Tilford explains that while trade imbalances are not, in theory, damaging to the global economy, the huge trade imbalances that have resulted from decreased consumption in the United States and United Kingdom, as well as the 2007 global financial crisis caused by over-leveraged banks, have created conditions that are unsustainable. To correct the problem, Tilford says, deficit countries such as the United States must save more and consume less, while at the same time surplus countries such as China must spend more and save less. In addition, Tilford concludes, currency exchange rates must be adjusted to further offset trade imbalances.

As you read, consider the following questions:

1. Why will it be disastrous if everybody saves more, according to Tilford?

2. How does Tilford indicate that China could discourage excess savings?

3. What robust steps are the Chinese taking to slow their economy, according to the viewpoint?

The developed world's slide into recession threatens an outbreak of protectionism. Unlike in 2008, governments now [in 2011] have few tools with which to combat a renewed economic downturn, which raises the likelihood of it developing into a slump. If so, protectionist pressure is certain to build. The country that moves first to erect trade barriers will no doubt take the blame for the resulting damage to the trading system. But the real villains will be the countries that skew their exchange policies, tax systems and industrial structures to gain export advantage. The irony is that the countries that are most dependent on free trade—those that produce more than they consume—are the biggest obstacle to a sustained recovery in the global economy. They need to change course before it is too late: All will suffer if countries move to erect new trade barriers, but the surplus economies will suffer most.

Surplus-country governments regularly exhort deficit countries to pay down debt, save more and 'live within their means'. But the real problem facing the global economy is an acute lack of aggregate demand. The world is awash with savings, but there is a dearth of profitable investment opportunities, which in turn reflects the weakness of consumption. The answer is not therefore for everybody to save more. This will be disastrous: It will further depress consumption and hence investment, and aggravate fiscal problems. If countries with big trade deficits (and correspondingly high levels of indebtedness) are to save more, surplus countries (those that live within their means) will have to save less and spend more.

Low Demand Is Now Offset by Reduced Supply or Greater Consumption

The weakness of domestic demand in the US, UK and across much of the eurozone is hitting global demand hard, but there is nothing to offset it. The big surplus countries—Germany, China and Japan—are not taking any steps to offset the contraction in demand elsewhere. Such a state of affairs is fraught with risk. If the world is to continue enjoying the benefits of global trade and finance, the global imbalances have to be unwound.

What are trade imbalances? A country's trade balance is a reflection of what it spends minus what it produces. In surplus countries, income exceeds their spending, so they lend the difference to countries where spending exceeds income, accumulating international assets in the process. Deficit countries are the flip side of this. They spend more than their income, borrowing from surplus countries to cover the difference, in the process accumulating international liabilities or debts. Export-led growth in surplus countries feeds (and is dependent on) debt-led growth in deficit countries. It is impossible for all countries to run surpluses, just as it is impossible for all to run deficits.

Huge Trade Imbalances Adversely Affect Capital Flows

Are trade imbalances sustainable? Trade imbalances and the accompanying capital flows between countries are not necessarily a problem. Fast-ageing wealthy societies tend to have excess savings and it makes sense to invest these in countries where domestic savings are insufficient to meet investment needs. Historically, this typically meant investing money in rapidly developing emerging markets. So long as current-account deficits remain modest and economies invest the corresponding capital inflows in ways that boost productivity growth, such imbalances are sustainable. But the imbalances we see today are of a different character. First, they are much bigger. The most egregious is that between China and the US, where still poor China is running a huge trade surplus with the US. Many of the other imbalances are between countries of broadly similar levels of economic development, such as those between members of the eurozone, or that between Japan and the US.

Imbalances of this scale and nature are far from benign. First, they lead to destabilising capital flows between economies. For example, the global financial crises of 2007 and the subsequent eurozone crisis were basically the result of capital flows between countries. Over-leveraged banks amplified the problem, but the underlying cause was outflows of capital from economies with excess savings in search of higher returns. Much as in the surplus economies themselves, the US, UK and the members of the eurozone that attracted large-scale capital inflows struggled to find productive uses for them: Rather than boosting productivity, the inflows pumped up asset prices and encouraged excessive household borrowing.

The imbalances survived both crises, and are now growing again from an already high level. This is clearly unsustainable. Unlike in the run-up to the financial crisis, the current situation has nothing do with excess demand in the deficit countries, but is taking place against a backdrop of stagnation and falling living standards in these economies. Households and firms in the deficit countries are saving more, but there has been no offsetting decline in private sector savings in the surplus countries. Against this kind of economic backdrop, trade deficits constitute a major drag on economic activity as they drain demand and employment, forcing governments to step in and fill the gap by running big fiscal deficits. The external demand upon which the surplus countries depend relies implicitly on unsustainable fiscal policies in the deficit countries.

Reducing Trade Imbalances Requires Opposite Actions in Deficit and Surplus Countries

How can imbalances be reduced? The deficit countries need a combination of higher net exports (export minus imports) and higher net savings (domestic savings minus domestic investment), while the surplus countries require the reverse. Put another way, the deficit countries need to get over their dependence on debt, surplus countries their addiction to exports. Deficit countries need more domestic savings and surplus countries more consumption.

Structural changes in both the surplus and deficit countries can clearly contribute to the necessary adjustments. Countries where expenditure lags output, such as Germany and Japan, could take steps to reverse the decline in wages and salaries as a proportion of national income. This would boost consumption, encourage more investment, and hence lower their corporate sectors' excess savings. For its part, China could discourage excess savings by reducing subsidies to its corporate sector, which is sitting on very large sums of cash. The Chinese authorities could also improve the country's social safety net and hence lower households' precautionary savings. However, such adjustments will take time, and time is in short supply. The only way to facilitate rapid adjustment is through shifts in relative prices.

There are three ways of bringing about these movements in prices, or shifts in countries' so-called 'real exchange rates'. The fate of the international trading system could depend on which is chosen. First, domestic prices can fall in the deficit countries. This comes about through declining costs and prices, as wages are cut and governments pursue fiscal austerity. Higher unemployment encourages households to save more, and the prices of imported goods rise relative to domestically produced ones.

This is basically what is being attempted in the eurozone. Trade imbalances are to be addressed by deflation in the deficit countries. Policy across the eurozone as a whole has a strongly deflationary bias, as much in the surplus economies as the deficit ones. This implies very weak economic growth, falls in prices (relative to the outside world) and higher unemployment. It also implies higher savings as governments tighten fiscal policy, companies sit on cash rather than investing it and fearful households boost their savings and rein in consumption. The risk is that the deficit countries' debt burdens will increase further (as the value of their debts grow, while their incomes fall), exacerbating their fiscal problems and undermining their ability to pay their creditors. Far from taking up some of the strain from the Americans, the eurozone is trying to run a big surplus with the rest of the world, adding to trade tensions.

Given how indebted the deficit countries are (in terms of public and private debt) rebalancing needs to take place through a combination of movements in nominal exchange rates (where possible) and somewhat higher inflation in the surplus countries. Very low interest rates and quantitative easing in the US is pushing up inflation in countries with currencies linked to the dollar—first and foremost China. The US has little option but to continue pumping dollars into its financial system, in order to compensate for the drag on its economy from the trade balance, and some of this money will continue to leak out to China. However, concerned at the rise in inflation, the Chinese authorities are taking robust steps to slow their economy by clamping down on the amount state-owned banks can lend. Easily the least damaging adjustment in the eurozone would be through higher inflation in Germany. But there is little sign of this. And if there were, the European Central Bank would raise interest rates.

Nominal Exchange Rate Changes Could Offset Trade Imbalances Somewhat

Finally, changes in relative prices can be brought about by movements in nominal exchange rates. For example, the Chinese could allow the renminbi to rise against the dollar or Germany could withdraw from the eurozone and reintroduce the D-mark, which would then appreciate sharply in value. Movements in nominal exchange rates offer by far the least damaging route to the needed rebalancing. It would avoid deflation in the deficit countries or inflation in the surplus ones.

The Chinese government is somewhat schizophrenic about the potential impact of renminbi revaluation. On the one hand, it maintains that it would not make any difference, because the deficits in countries like America reflect the latter's lack of savings, which would not be affected by an appreciation of the Chinese currency. On the other hand, it argues that a stronger renminbi would hit the Chinese economy hard and be disastrous for global economic growth. In short, the Chinese government is dependent on others running up debt, but at the same time condemns them for doing so. Movements in nominal exchange rates may yet be the mechanism by which the German trade surplus is cut. The current eurozone strategy of deflation in the deficit economies rather than reflation in Germany threatens to force economies out of the currency union. This would open the way for a rebalancing of the German economy, but at enormous political and economic cost to Europe.

Surplus-country governments, notably the Chinese and German ones, often warn of the risks of protectionism. They fail to make the connection between the structures of their economies and the trade deficits (and rising indebtedness) of others. As a result, they are the real threat to the international trading order. If the US cannot rebalance its economy and get it growing sustainably, there is a real risk it will opt for protectionism. Other countries with big trade deficits could quickly follow suit. The resulting rebalancing would be brutal for the surplus countries, and many of the benefits of global trade and finance would be lost. To prevent this, the G20 [a group of twenty finance ministers and central bank governors] needs to agree on a global strategy to rebalance demand. This would require the surplus economies to acknowledge that they are part of the problem and to develop strategies to reduce their export dependence.

Periodical and Internet Sources Bibliography

The following articles have been selected to supplement the diverse views presented in this chapter.

Max Baucus	"Hearing Statement of Senator Max Baucus (D-Mont.) Regarding the US-Korea Free Trade Agreement," US Senate Committee on Finance, May 26, 2011. www.finance.senate.gov.
Bloomberg News	"US Presses China on Value of Its Currency," *New York Times*, May 3, 2012.
Citizen.org	"The NAFTA Clone 'Free Trade' Deal with Korea Threatening Jobs, the Economy, Security & the Environment," January 2011. www.citizen.org.
Global Trade Watch	"Korea-US Free Trade Agreement (FTA): Problematic Foreign Investor and Financial Deregulation Provisions," July 2011. www.tradewatch.org.
Maurice R. Greenberg	"Time for a China-US Free Trade Agreement," *Wall Street Journal*, January 9, 2012.
Kathleen Hennessey	"Despite Divisiveness, Congress Passes 3 Trade Pacts," *Los Angeles Times*, October 13, 2011.
Annie Lowrey	"An Increase in Barriers to Trade Is Reported," *New York Times*, June 22, 2012.
Demetrios Marantis	"Testimony of Ambassador Demetrios Marantis, Senate Committee on Finance Hearing on the US-Korea Free Trade Agreement," May 26, 2011. www.finance.senate.gov.
Ricardo Martinelli	"Pact Between US, Panama Will Further Strengthen Nations' Ties," *The Hill*, March 18, 2010.

For Further Discussion

Chapter 1

1. Robert E. Scott contends that free trade leads to American job loss, but Daniel J. Ikenson and Scott Lincicome state the opposite, contending that removing barriers to trade is the way to long-term economic recovery. What are the strengths and weaknesses of each argument? Whose argument is stronger? Why?

2. Ian Fletcher states that free trade agreements (FTAs) are bad news for the American economy. What does Fletcher see as the greatest disadvantage of FTAs? Do you agree or disagree with Fletcher's arguments? Use text from the viewpoint to support your reasoning.

Chapter 2

1. Many proponents of free trade state that free trade is good for the poor and is a means of alleviating poverty. But David T. Rowlands believes that free trade hurts the poor and leaves them no choice but to pursue illegal activities. Explain how, according to Rowlands, free trade leads to increased criminal activity, in Mexico in particular. Do you agree with Rowlands' assessment? Why or why not?

2. Nicole J. Hassoun argues that free trade can lessen both poverty and environmental threats. She explains that "it is important to link free trade agreements both to provisions to reduce poverty and to provisions to mitigate environmental problems." After reading Hassoun's viewpoint, do you think it's possible for free trade to have a beneficial impact on poverty and the environment? Explain your reasoning.

Chapter 3

1. Samuel Gregg believes that free trade must be encouraged, and that all barriers to free trade must cease, if the world economy is to get back on an even keel. However, Max Fisher believes that free trade exploits women and child laborers. What are the strengths of Gregg's argument? What are the strengths of Fisher's argument? With which opinion do you agree, and why?

2. Michelle Chen writes that free trade agreements cause suffering for people in Colombia who favor union rights and oppose free trade with the United States until and unless changes are made to protect union workers who fight for labor rights and protection. Do you think there is a common ground that can be found between labor activists and those who are proponents of free trade, and what might that common ground be? If you think there can be no common ground, explain your reasoning.

Chapter 4

1. Meredith Kolsky Lewis writes about the Trans-Pacific Partnership (TPP). How does the TPP differ from other free trade agreements into which the United States has entered, particularly in terms of numbers of countries involved? Lewis argues that the United States is interested in even more nations joining the partnership. For what reasons is this desirable to the United States, in terms of US engagement in the Asia-Pacific region? Do you think that the TPP is a good idea for the US economy? Why or why not?

2. Simon Tilford contends that the world economy's slide into recession will prompt an outbreak of protectionism among many nations. But Tilford says that "surplus-country governments, notably the Chinese and German ones, often warn of the risks of protectionism." Why

would these nations resist protectionism? And what is the real threat to the international trading order? Do you agree with Tilford's assessment? Why or why not?

Organizations to Contact

The editors have compiled the following list of organizations concerned with the issues debated in this book. The descriptions are derived from materials provided by the organizations. All have publications or information available for interested readers. The list was compiled on the date of publication of the present volume; the information provided here may change. Be aware that many organizations take several weeks or longer to respond to inquiries, so allow as much time as possible.

American Cause
PO Box 7, Vienna, VA   22183
(703) 255-2632 • fax: (703) 255-2219
e-mail: americancause@gmail.com
website: www.theamericancause.org

Economic patriotism is a main theme of the work of the American Cause, a foundation founded by conservative columnist Patrick Buchanan. The foundation believes that any trade policy must include maintaining the United States' manufacturing base as a priority. The website contains a collection of Buchanan's columns on trade, including "Free Trade and Funny Math," as well as columns on other issues.

Cato Institute
1000 Massachusetts Avenue NW
Washington, DC   20001-5403
(202) 842-0200 • fax: (202) 842-3490
website: www.cato.org

Libertarian think tank the Cato Institute works to highlight what it sees as the benefits of free trade. Among these perceived benefits are wider consumer choice and better American-made goods due to pressure from foreign competition. The institute takes a dim view of government interference of any kind with the economy, including restrictions on trade and on immigration. It publishes a frequent *Free Trade Bulletin* and briefing papers such as "Race to the Bottom? The Presidential Candidates' Positions on Trade."

Competitive Enterprise Institute
1899 L Street NW, 12th Floor, Washington, DC 20036
(202) 331-1010 • fax: (202) 331-0640
e-mail: info@cei.org
website: http://cei.org

The Competitive Enterprise Institute focuses on proposing policies that would make US businesses more competitive in the world market. The group promotes free trade, which it sees as under attack from special interests. Policy papers such as "The Greening of Trade Policy: 'Sustainable Development' and Global Trade" and transcribed congressional testimony by its experts are available on the group's website.

Economic Policy Institute
1333 H Street NW, Suite 300, East Tower
Washington, DC 20005-4707
(202) 775-8810 • fax: (202) 775-0819
e-mail: epi@epi.org
website: www.epi.org

The Economic Policy Institute states that its mission is "to inform people and empower them to seek solutions that will ensure broadly shared prosperity and opportunity." The nonprofit, nonpartisan think tank is particularly concerned with improving economic opportunity for working Americans. Its website hosts papers such as "Costly Trade with China" and "Outsourcing America's Technology and Knowledge Jobs," as well as collections of economic data.

European Free Trade Association (EFTA)
EFTA Secretariat, Geneva (Headquarters)
9-11, rue de Varembé, Geneva 20 1211
  Switzerland
+41 22 332 26 00 • fax: +41 22 332 26 77

e-mail: mail.gva@efta.int
website: www.efta.int

The European Free Trade Association (EFTA) is an intergovernmental organization set up for the promotion of free trade and economic integration to the benefit of its four member states: Iceland, Liechtenstein, Norway, and Switzerland. EFTA has responsibility for the management of the EFTA convention; the Agreement on the European Economic Area; and EFTA's worldwide network of free trade and partnership agreements. Its website hosts numerous publications, among them are fact sheets about the organization and about global trade that focus on specific regions or nations, and EFTA bulletins, which have information on economic strategies and the advantages and disadvantages of free trade.

Federation of International Trade Associations (FITA)
172 Fifth Avenue #118, Brooklyn, NY   11217
(703) 634-3482
e-mail: info@fita.org
website: www.fita.org

The Federation of International Trade Associations (FITA), founded in 1984, fosters international trade by strengthening the role of local, regional, national, and global associations that have an international mission. FITA provides resources, benefits, and services to the international trade community and useful tools to help individuals do business globally. Among its resources are trade publications, which cover a variety of topics, and useful links associated with international trade, including geography information and maps.

Foundation for Economic Education (FEE)
30 South Broadway, Irvington-on-Hudson, NY   10533
(914) 591-7230 • fax: (914) 591-8910
e-mail: info@fee.org
website: www.fee.org

The Foundation for Economic Education (FEE) is one of the oldest organizations dedicated to spreading the message of the free market to students and citizens. The foundation works to counter what it sees as anti–free market beliefs. It publishes three periodicals, the *Freeman, Notes from FEE,* and *In Brief.*

Global Development and Environment Institute at Tufts University (GDAE)

44 Teele Avenue, Somerville, MA   02144
(617) 627-3530 • fax: (617) 627-2409
e-mail: GDAE@tufts.edu
website: www.ase.tufts.edu/gdae/

The Global Development and Environment Institute (GDAE) combines expertise in economics, policy, science, and technology in researching social and environmental trends in the developing world. Its website features articles such as "Free Trade Agreements in the Americas: Worth the Investment?" and "Multinationals and the 'Maquila Mindset' in Mexico's Silicon Valley."

Global Exchange

2017 Mission Street, 2nd Floor, San Francisco, CA   94110
(415) 255-7296 • fax: (415) 255-7498
e-mail: web@globalexchange.org
website: www.globalexchange.org

Global Exchange is an international human rights organization that promotes social, economic, and environmental justice worldwide. The organization is concerned with fair trade and the exploitation of sweat shop labor in developing countries. Its website includes information and contacts for activism as well as a sign-up page for the group's monthly newsletter. Its articles include "Top Ten Reasons to Oppose the Free Trade Area of the Americas" and "10 Ways to Democratize the Global Economy."

Global Trade Watch (GTW)

215 Pennsylvania Avenue SE, Washington, DC   20003
(202) 546-4996

e-mail: gtwinfo@citizen.org
website: www.tradewatch.org

Global Trade Watch (GTW) is a division of the nonprofit consumer advocacy organization Public Citizen. Global Trade Watch's mission is to ensure that in this era of globalization, a majority of individuals have the opportunity to enjoy economic security, a clean environment, safe food, medicines, and other products; access to quality affordable services such as health care; and the exercise of democratic decision making about the matters that affect their lives. GTW serves as researcher and translator of an array of globalization issues for other nongovernmental organizations, the press, policy makers, and the public. Their publications include fact sheets and talking points on current campaigns; charts of how each member of Congress voted on each major trade vote since 1991; tables summarizing the outcomes of various free trade agreements; and copies of annotated trade pact texts.

International Trade Administration (ITA)
US Department of Commerce, 1401 Constitution Avenue NW
Washington, DC 20230
(800) 872-8723
website: www.trade.gov

The mission of the International Trade Administration (ITA) is to promote prosperity through trade, investment, and enhancing American competitiveness. The agency's website contains links to policy documents concerning trade, including the text of free trade agreements and the administration's newsletter, *International Trade Update*.

**Organisation for Economic Co-operation
and Development (OECD)**
2 Rue André Pascal, Paris Cedex 16   75775
   France
+33 1 45 24 82 00 • fax: +33 1 45 24 85 00
website: www.oecd.org

The Organisation for Economic Co-operation and Development (OECD) is an organization of governments committed to democracy and a free market economy. It fosters cooperation among the richer nations in the world in channeling their assistance to poorer nations. Its chief publication is the annual *OECD Factbook*, and it produces reports such as "Regional Trade Agreements Can Be Good for the Environment."

Peterson Institute for International Economics
1750 Massachusetts Avenue NW, Washington, DC   20036
(202) 328-9000 • fax: (202) 659-3225
e-mail: comments@petersoninstitute.org
website: www.iie.com

According to its website, the Peterson Institute for International Economics is one of the few think tanks that is widely regarded as neutral and nonpartisan by Congress and the press. Generally supportive of free trade, the institute's publications also recognize the importance of American competitiveness. The institute's website contains a wide variety of policy briefs, such as "Strengthening Trade Adjustment Assistance" and "Fear and Offshoring: The Scope and Potential Impact of Imports and Exports of Services," as well as links to books available for purchase.

**United Nations Conference on Trade
and Development (UNCTAD)**
Palais des Nations 8-14, Av. de la Paix, Geneva 10   1211
   Switzerland
+41 22 917 1234 • fax: +41 22 917 0057
e-mail: info@unctad.org
website: www.unctad.org

The United Nations Conference on Trade and Development (UNCTAD) assists developing countries in benefiting from global trade. Areas of concern include the negotiation of equitable trade treaties and international trade's effect on the environment. UNCTAD's website has numerous publications such as the annual *World Investment Report*.

World Trade Organization (WTO)

Centre William Rappard, Geneva 21   CH-1211
   Switzerland
+ 41 (0)22 739 51 11 • fax: + 41 (0)22 731 42 06
e-mail: enquiries@wto.org
website: www.wto.org

The World Trade Organization (WTO) is the only international organization charged with setting the rules for global
trade. The group provides a forum for countries and regions
to negotiate the terms of worldwide trade. Its website provides
a wealth of trade statistics as well as its annual trade report,
which offers a comprehensive overview of WTO trade activities that took place throughout the year.

Bibliography of Books

Tom Barry — *Zapata's Revenge: Free Trade and the Farm Crisis in Mexico.* Boston, MA: South End Press, 1999.

Jagdish Bhagwati — *In Defense of Globalization.* New York: Oxford University Press, 2007.

Sherrod Brown — *Myths of Free Trade: Why American Trade Policy Has Failed.* New York: New Press, 2004.

Ha-Joon Chang — *Bad Samaritans: The Myth of Free Trade and the Secret History of Capitalism.* New York: Bloomsbury Press, 2008.

Paul Collier — *The Bottom Billion: Why the Poorest Countries Are Failing and What Can Be Done About It.* New York: Oxford University Press, 2007.

Tyler Cowen — *Creative Destruction: How Globalization Is Changing the World's Cultures.* Princeton, NJ: Princeton University Press, 2002.

Daniel W. Drezner — *US Trade Strategy: Free Versus Fair.* New York: Council on Foreign Relations, 2006.

William Easterly — *The White Man's Burden: Why the West's Efforts to Aid the Rest Have Done So Much Ill and So Little Good.* New York: Oxford University Press, 2007.

Ian Fletcher   *Free Trade Doesn't Work: What Should Replace It and Why?* Washington, DC: US Business & Industry Council, 2011.

Jeffrey A. Frieden   *Global Capitalism: Its Fall and Rise in the Twentieth Century.* New York: W.W. Norton & Company, 2007.

Douglas A. Irwin   *Free Trade Under Fire.* Princeton, NJ: Princeton University Press, 2009.

Remy Jurenas   *Agriculture in the US Free Trade Agreements: Trade with Current and Prospective Partners, Impact and Issues.* Hauppauge, NY: Nova Science Pub. Inc., 2008.

Jane Kelsey   *No Ordinary Deal: Unmasking the Trans-Pacific Partnership Free Trade Agreement.* Crows Nest, New South Wales: Allen & Unwin, 2011.

Peter W. Navarro and Greg Autry   *Death by China: Confronting the Dragon—A Global Call to Action.* Upper Saddle River, NJ: Prentice Hall, 2011.

Eul-Soo Pang   *The US-Singapore Free Trade Agreement: An American Perspective on Power, Trade, and Security in the Asia Pacific.* Singapore: Institute of Southeast Asian Studies, 2011.

Pietra Rivoli — *The Travels of a T-Shirt in the Global Economy: An Economist Examines the Markets, Power, and Politics of World Trade.* Hoboken, NJ: John Wiley, 2009.

Andrew Ross — *Fast Boat to China: Corporate Flight and the Consequences of Free Trade—Lessons from Shanghai.* New York: Pantheon Books, 2006.

William Shearer — *The Conservative Case Against Free Trade.* Vienna, VA: The Conservative Caucus Foundation, 2012.

Robert Sirico — *Defending the Free Market: The Moral Case for a Free Economy.* Washington, DC: Regnery Publishing, 2012.

Joseph E. Stiglitz — *Freefall: America, Free Markets, and the Sinking of the World Economy.* New York: W.W. Norton & Co., 2010.

Joseph E. Stiglitz — *Making Globalization Work.* New York: W.W. Norton & Co., 2007.

Linda Weiss, Elizabeth Thurbon, and John Mathews — *How to Kill a Country: Australia's Devastating Trade Deal with the United States.* Crows Nest, New South Wales: Allen & Unwin, 2004.

Index

V

W

CPSIA information can be obtained
at www.ICGtesting.com
Printed in the USA
FFOW020654180213
888FF